TO GIVE ONE'S LIFE FOR THE WORK OF ANOTHER

LUIGI GIUSSANI

To Give One's Life
for the Work
of Another

Edited by Julián Carrón

McGill-Queen's University Press
Montreal & Kingston • London • Chicago

© McGill-Queen's University Press 2022

ISBN 978-0-2280-1048-7 (cloth)
ISBN 978-0-2280-1165-1 (paper)
ISBN 978-0-2280-1049-4 (ePDF)
ISBN 978-0-2280-1050-0 (ePUB)

Legal deposit first quarter 2022
Bibliothèque nationale du Québec

Printed in Canada on acid-free paper that is 100% ancient forest free
(100% post-consumer recycled), processed chlorine free

Reprinted 2022

Translations:
1997   Patrick Stevenson
1998   Patrick Stevenson / Amanda Murphy
1999   Amanda Murphy
2000   Patrick Stevenson
2001   Susan Scott / Edo Mörlin
2002   Susan Scott / Edo Mörlin
2004   Susan Scott / Edo Mörlin
Introductions and editorial note: Kristin Hurd
Text revised by Laura Ferrario

_____

Library and Archives Canada Cataloguing in Publication

Title: To give one's life for the work of another / Luigi Giussani ; preface by
Julián Carrón.
Names: Giussani, Luigi, author. | Carrón Pérez, Julián, writer of preface.
Identifiers: Canadiana (print) 20210377712 | Canadiana (ebook) 20210377909
   | ISBN 9780228011651 (paper) | ISBN 9780228010487 (cloth) | ISBN
   9780228010494 (ePDF) | ISBN 9780228010500 (ePUB)
Subjects: LCSH: Comunione e liberazione. | LCSH: Spiritual exercises.
   | LCSH: Spiritual life—Catholic Church.
Classification: LCC BX2182.3.G58 2022 | DDC 248.4/82—dc23

_____

This book was typeset in 10.5/13 Sabon.

Contents

"Christ Is the Life of My Life"

What defines the historical context in which we are immersed? The prevalence of ethics over ontology.[1] This was the judgment Giussani formulated at the end of the 1990s. He saw it as the culmination of a process that began centuries before, with modernity and the spread of the influence of rationalism, which transformed cultural and political attitudes toward Christianity and the Church. From that point forward, the primacy of ethics over ontology became a general norm. In the wake of the separation and hierarchization of mathematical-scientific knowledge and philosophical (and religious) knowledge, the way of conceiving of life and reality was more and more determined by behaviours, by preferences: not by reason, the way reality makes itself evident in experience; in other words, by ontology, but ethically – by a behavioural norm, based on which a person uses reason.[2] "The Church, too, attacked by rationalism, stressed ethics to the people and in her theology, taking ontology for granted and almost obliterating its originating force." (see p. 10)

Perceiving the growing contrasts with the state and emerging cultural forms, much of the Church began to speak to what others – including detractors – could understand or had to agree upon: basic ethics and moral values. They neglected the dogmatic content of Christianity, its ontology; in other words, the announcement that God became man and that this event continues in history through a human reality – the Church, the "tangible Body of Christ" (p. 107) – made up of people who document the fullness of life Christ brings about in the lives of those who recognize and follow Him. As a consequence, the Church's preaching also began to mostly focus on ethical appeals: Christianity began to be proposed in a way that was first and foremost about duty, rather than attraction. When that happens, faith loses its reasonability and its capacity to generate life in the Christian people.

It seemed the obvious and easiest way to retain a hold on people was to appeal to Catholic morality. It was not deemed necessary to give sufficient reasons a person should follow the Church. They thought insisting upon a few basic behavioural norms would be enough to get their audience to follow along. In this way, the Church could continue to exercise its function as a moral beacon. As long as the cultural context was homogeneous and the Church played the role of a primary actor, the morality born from Christian culture, though it earned less and less consensus, still held up. When the social context become more diverse and multicultural, however, everything changed. The process of erosion that had begun was suddenly accelerated. It was striking for me when, recently, I saw images of churches that had been transformed into night clubs, movie theatres, tennis courts, and swimming pools. Hunkering down on a defence of morals – though correct in its principals – did not stand up to the contrary mentality running rampant, gaining more and more ground and imposing new values and new rights.

By not proposing itself at the level of ontology, as a living event capable of corresponding to man's deepest desires, a Christianity reduced to morals progressively lost all attraction. Consequently, many of our contemporaries are born and live indifferent to Christianity and to faith. It is as if there has been a lack of familiarity with humanity, due to a naivety regarding "what it is that can move us most deeply."[3] Having neglected humanity's deepest needs – for truth, beauty, justice, and happiness – the Church appeared to be increasingly distant from daily life, and faith seemed ultimately incomprehensible.

How have we come to this point? To that question, Giussani gives a reply that sheds light on our present, as well as our past. The process began, he asserts, "without anyone realizing it," in "a separation of the meaning of life from experience." God comes to be seen as separate from experience, as having no impact on life. "In other words, the meaning of life has no longer any relationship or has a relationship that is difficult to define with the moment of existence in which one is actually walking." This, however, depends – and here Giussani takes a fundamental step – on something that already happened before: "The heart of the matter becomes clear in the dispute over how to read and analyze the relationship between reason and experience." (p. 45) At the root of this divorce, of the separation between God and experience, then, there is another reduction at the level of knowledge, related to the way one conceives of the relationship between reason and experience.

What does Giussani mean by experience? "Experience is the emergence of reality to man's consciousness; it is reality becoming transparent to man's gaze. So reality is something that you come across, it is a datum, and reason is that level of creation in which creation becomes aware of itself." It is, therefore, in experience that reality reveals itself, and it reveals itself as something given, not produced by us, that points us beyond itself to something that is its ultimate origin. Reason is the gaze before which that revelation occurs; it is the level of reality in which reality becomes aware of itself as coming from somewhere else. Giussani observes, "Jean Guitton, by indentifying us to be in this restless unease of ours, encouraged us, to make us feel the correctness of our attitude as regards the relationship between reason and life when he said, 'to be reasonable is to subject reason to experience.'" (p. 46) Why is this act of submission reasonable? Because, if experience is the place reality becomes transparent, then reason is at the service of that transparency, it is its instrument.

Having arrived at this point, the next step Giussani makes is not surprising. "In order to defend God in his truth and in order to defend the need for man to conceive his life as His and to tend in everything to please this supreme creator and manager of all that exists, we need to recover the word reason from our heart." (p. 46) If, in fact, "the word reason is used wrongly," if one begins to think of it as the "measure" of reality, all of human knowledge, the entire human adventure, is compromised.

"If reason is understood as measure of reality – and this always implies reason as a preconception [...] –, there are three possible serious reductions that affect all our behaviour in life." (p. 46) These do not just refer to the past, but to our current attitude. Let's look at them.

a) "First reduction – I am describing the genesis of our behaviour in its dramatic and contradictory aspect: ideology in place of an Event."

What are the implications of this substitution? Man can either relate
to reality through an initiative inspired by what happening, by what he
perceives in himself through the impact of what happens, or through
an initiative that obscures, that tends to distort what happens, obeying something that "does not spring from his own way of reacting to
the things he meets, the things he comes across, but from preconceptions." The starting point, then, is "a particular impression of things,
a particular evaluation of things, a particular attitude one takes up
before tackling things, above all before judging them." Suppose, Giussani expounds, that there is a mining or railway accident: the way
one tackles these events that question man tends "not to be born, of a
human reverberation, of what man feels as man before these events."
It is as if an argument he has already heard, a preconception, inserts
itself in his judgment: "he starts from a preconception. So it is that
the liberal- or republican-biased newspaper will report it in one way,
while the newspaper favouring the government will take a different
view." Now, a preconception, that starting point for a person's action,
in order to go down in history and endure in time, "to score points
in the fields of public opinion and the judgment of society, needs to
be developed. Its development is through the logic of a discourse that
becomes ideology. The logic of a discourse that starts off from a preconception and wants to impose it is called ideology." (p. 47–8)

This is the battle each of us engages in, with greater or lesser awareness, each day. Christians, too, like everyone in our historical context,
cannot escape facing this choice, this battle: "Our Christian life, our
faith, and our concrete morality, the set-up of our lives is determined
either by current ideologies or by the factuality, the supremacy of our
existence, of things as they happen, of things as we come across them,
of things to which you react in a given way, of facts: facts as events."
(p. 48) Just as when a baby is born: it imposes itself on everyone with
the disarming power of its mere presence; it was not there before but
now it exists. In short, it is an event.

How, then, can we fully live the relationship with reality in a sustained way, with a constant tension, being defined "by the supremacy
[…] of things as they happen?" Giussani responds: "There are events
that are great and events that are of the tiniest significance." In order
for us to live reality intensely, we must be touched by a great event,
an origin and "founding principle of the whole of human experience," which is present. Human experience cannot be founded on
something stuck in the past. This observation helps us understand

how critical it is that we grasp the nature of Christianity, since it is continually at risk of being reduced to ideology, which is its exact opposite. "Christianity is an event and is therefore present, it is present now, and its characteristic is that it is present as a memory, and Christian memory is not the same as a remembrance, or better, it is not a remembrance, but the re-happening of the Presence itself." Christianity can only be decisive for living men and women, thus changing the way they face everything, when it is an event, and is recognized and followed as such. "Only the recognition of this event prevents us from being slaves to any ideology." (p. 48–9)

b) After underlining this first point, Giussani identifies the second reduction that influences our behaviour. "In so far as [man] gives in to the dominant ideologies that emerge from the common mentality, [there is...] a separation [...] between sign and appearance, and as a consequence the reduction of sign to appearance. The more we realize what a sign is, the more we understand how vile and disastrous it is to reduce a sign to appearance." (p. 49)

But what is a sign? Giussani describes it as, "the experience of a factor, a presence in reality that refers to something else. A sign is an experienceable reality whose meaning is another reality, a reality that can be experienced; it acquires its meaning by leading to another reality." Once again, the proper use of reason is in play: "To exhaust the experience of the sign by interpreting it only in its perceptively immediate aspect or appearance" is unreasonable, because that appearance "does not tell the whole experience of the things we are looking at." Yet we easily fall into this temptation, almost without realizing it: "A certain attitude of spirit makes you behave more or less like this towards the reality of the world and of existence (the circumstances, the relationship with things, to start a family, bring up your children): it feels the rub, blocking your human capacity to search for meaning that our relationship with reality inevitably solicits in our intelligence." When the capacity of our intelligence to search for meaning is blocked, we end up with the "destitution"[4] of what is visible, to use Finkelkraut's term. It is the "emptying of what we see, of what we touch, of what we perceive," affirming that "what happens, happens just because it happens, avoiding the shock, the need to look at the present in its relationship with the whole." (p. 49–50)

In contrast, Giussani acutely asserts, "the concept of sign [...] operationally brings the meaning of things into life"; it leads reason to the ultimate depth of reality. Here Giussani introduces a very courageous affirmation: "Mystery (in other words, God) and sign (in other words, contingent reality in as much as it always recalls something else: even the tiniest stone, in order to be itself, has to be conceived of as made by God, has to be a reminder of the source of Being), [...] in a certain sense coincide." What does he mean? "The Mystery is the depth of the sign, the sign points to the presence of the deep Mystery, of God the Creator and the Redeemer, of God the Father. The sign [...] points out to our eyes the presence of something Other, of the deep Mystery for all things, it points it out to our eyes, to our ears, to our hands." In other words, "The Mystery becomes an experience through the sign." (p. 50)

Recognizing things as signs of the Mystery and grasping the value of all things in as much as they recall Another is proper to the nature of reason. Yet ideology presents itself as the tendency to call concrete only those things that are apparent, that you can see, feel, and touch. That is the still the operating framework, despite the clamorous collapse of the great ideologies of the twentieth century.

c) This is where the third reduction comes in: "The elimination of the value of sign implies – I don't know whether more as a cause or an effect – the reduction of the heart to feelings." The heart is no longer the ultimate motor, the deep driver of human action, the criterion for reason's judgment, the place of the wonder and affective energy that constitute our original relationship of knowledge with reality; feelings take over in its place. "This is precisely how our responsibility becomes irresponsible: we give in and use our feelings in place of our heart," when instead the latter "acts as the fundamental factor of the human personality. Feelings do not, because taken on their own feelings act as a reactivity, after all they are animalistic." (p. 52) Cesare Pavese wrote, "I do not yet understand what the tragedy of existence may be [...], but this point is so clear. I must overcome this luxurious indulgence and stop regarding states of soul as an end in themselves."[5]

For Giussani, "the heart indicates the unity of feeling and reason. It implies a concept of reason that is not blocked, a reason according to the full extent of its own possibility: reason cannot act without what is called affectivity. It is the heart, as reason and affectivity, which is the condition necessary for the healthy realization of reason. The condition necessary in order for reason to be reason is that affectivity take hold of it and thus move the whole man. Reason and feelings, reason and affectivity: this is man's heart." (p. 52–3) What a gaze we see constantly witnessed in Giussani, one that takes all the factors of humanity into account! I am amazed each time, because in reading him I am always confronted with an intelligence of reality that does not stop at the surface, but rather penetrates to the depths. There is never a time he fails to grasp all the dynamics of the relationship of the I with the world in which it lives.

How can we escape from these reductions? By merely discussing them? By exerting all our effort to reverse the tendency? No – the answer Giussani gives leads us back to the level of an experience within anyone's grasp – it takes encountering a lived humanity that cannot be reduced to these, a presence that frees the I from the cage it has built around itself, shattering the measuring stick of appearances and breaking the chain of reactive actions to make us "live always the real intensely,"[6] to use that expression found in the tenth chapter of *The Religious Sense* once again.

Here, the nature of Christianity emerges, just as it was made evident at its origin: "Jesus was a man like all the others, He was a man with nothing exceptional to the definition of man, a man like all the others. But Jesus said things of Himself that others didn't say; He said things and acted in a way that others didn't. The Sign of all signs. Once people got to know His reality, once they were struck by His claim, they looked at Him and treated Him as the sign of someone else, He was the reminder of something else. How clearly we see in John's gospel that Jesus did not see the attractiveness He had for the others as referring ultimately to Himself, but to the Father; the attraction was to Himself, but so that He could lead people to the Father, as awareness and obedience!" (p. 59–60) That ultimate reality recalled by all of reality (every sign) became a man, "The Sign of all signs"; a man who walked down the street, with whom you could eat, speak, and whom you could follow: this is the Christian event, the content of the announcement proclaimed to the hearts of men and women.

In this book, there are pages in which Giussani invites us to put ourselves in the place of those who first met that young man who was so different from all others, and the beginning of their faith: "Faith in Christ, as it appears clearly at the birth of the Christian fact, is knowing a Presence as something exceptional, being struck by it and then adhering to what He says of Himself. It is a fact; it is a fact that made it possible for Christianity to erupt into the world. Now we want nothing else but to know and live what happened." (p. 60)

Faith is recognizing an exceptional presence, recognizing the divine present in a determined human reality. It is, therefore, "an act that has reason as its starting point [...] reason as the affirmation that the Mystery is a reality that exists, without which man cannot begin to look reasonably at reality. In other words, the starting point for faith is reason as awareness of reality, that is man's religious sense." (p. 60)

Faith is not an emotion; it is "not a changing feeling that identifies the existence of God as it wants and lives religiosity as it likes. It's a judgment that affirms a reality – a present Mystery." Giussani describes the nature of faith with spectacular words: "Faith is rational, since it flourishes at the extreme boundary of the dynamics of reason like a flower of grace to which man adheres with his freedom." How can our freedom adhere to this flower that "cannot be understood as to its origin and manufacture?" By following, "with simplicity, what his reason perceives as being exceptional, with that immediate certainty, as happens with the unassailable and indestructible evidence of factors and moments of reality, as they enter the horizon of your own person." (p. 60–1)

We need to keep this suggestion from Giussani well in mind: that the event of Christ is something exceptional, "but in order to grasp it in its newness, reason has to accept it at once with simplicity and recognize what happens, and what has happened, with the immediate certainty that one has towards any evidence of reality." Christ offers himself to our freedom; he does not impose upon it. It is the same as happened in the beginning: "Before everything else, before the judgment that John gives about that Man, that Peter gives about that Man, before their judgment and adherence, first of all there is this simplicity, this simple heart, these simple eyes, this tension, this simple desire that is open to assimilate, that is able to assimilate with clarity what it has encountered, that aspect of reality that it has come across." (p. 61) To intercept, to recognize and to follow the truth made present in the sign of a humanity that is different and attractive, we do not need any special gift, but only this simplicity of heart.

Then Cardinal Ratzinger, in reference to the social context at the time – a varied, multicultural one; one in which, as I said before, many churches were turned into night clubs, movie theatres, tennis courts, or pools – asked himself, "Why has faith still any chance at all?" He was thinking of young believers, who are culturally mature. He answers, "I should say it is because it corresponds to the nature of man [...]. The longing for the infinite is alive and unquenchable within man. None of the attempted answers will do; only the God who himself became finite in order to tear open our finitude and lead us out into the wide spaces of his infinity, only he corresponds to the question of our being."[7] All it takes is coming across the fact of Christianity, Christianity according to its original nature: a contemporary event in the form of a human encounter. Its reduction to moralism or the mere verbal repetition of the announcement are not capable of responding to our original needs. In the same way, neither is its – rationalistic – reduction to one of the many expressions of the religious sense, to one of the many forms of religiosity.

Now, "in the modern era, by losing the true nature of reason, rationalism makes confusion between religious sense and faith quite habitual, thus emptying faith of its true nature." This did not happen without negative consequences for contemporary man, and not just for Christians. "The confusion between religious sense and faith makes everything confused. The collapse of faith in its true nature, as it is in Tradition, that is, in the life of the Church, the collapse of faith as recognition of 'Christ is all in all,' as identification with Christ, and imitation of Christ, has given rise to the present-day bewilderment, which reveals itself in various, identifiable aspects." (p. 62)

In 1998, Giussani described these aspects of present-day bewilderment, the traces of which we can find in our own lives and those of the people around us. The Christian fact, the Presence that faith recognizes can be reduced and emptied of its historicity and concreteness, but then Christian faith becomes a caricature, meaning it becomes unreasonable and incomprehensible because it is deprived of its foundation in reality. This is the fruit of what Giussani called the "Five Withouts" of modern rationalism. We will briefly review them.

a) "The first consequence of rationalism can be summarized in the formula: 'God without Christ.' It is the denial of the fact that it is only through Christ that God be revealed to us for what He is."

(p. 61) Without Christ, however, faith loses its reasonability and becomes *fideism*: the foundation of the Christian experience falls apart and moral efforts lack adequate motivation. God goes back to being an object constructed by human thought and imagination, according to different cultural or ethical emphases.

b) The second consequence of rationalism is, "Christ without the Church," meaning Christ without His Body, without His flesh. This is gnosis, or Gnosticism, in all its forms. "If you eliminate from Christ the fact of being a man, a real, historical man, then the possibility of a Christian experience [...] is also eliminated." Christianity is a human experience, "so it is made of time and space just like every reality that is also material. If this aspect of the materiality of the object is lacking from the experience that man has of Christ, then the possibility of Christ's contemporaneity is also lacking, that is the truth of what He said of Himself." The rationalistic position will not allow for a particular reality, made up of time and space, to be "the place that gives rise to the experience of man's ultimate meaning: man's ultimate meaning is not part of day-to-day experience." (p. 63)

Christ, Giussani continually underlines, is not an idea but a real presence, one you can hear, see and touch. Where? In a historical phenomenon: the life of the Church. "You cannot think of Christ without such a concreteness; it would be a reduction and a transformation of what Christ said about Himself, of what Christ is, as the revealer, in the hands of God. Tertullian affirms, "*Caro cardo salutis*" (The flesh is the hinge of salvation)." (p. 63)

c) A third result of the influence of a rationalist mentality on the personal and community life of the Church is a "Church without the world," the consequences of which are "clericalism and spiritualism [...], a twofold reduction of the value of the Church as the Body of Christ." (p. 64)

d) Giussani goes another step, introducing a fourth without: "If the Church is without the world, then this world tends to be without an I: in other words, it is an alienation. This world is characterized by alienation as the end result, whether foreseen or not, whether wanted or not – normally wanted by the power, by whoever has the cultural power in that moment. Alienation." (p. 68)

The final result of that alienation achieved by those in power is "the loss of freedom, the non-recognition or the abolition of freedom, an abolition not proclaimed theoretically, but in effect put in operation." Seeing as freedom, however you wish to define it, is "the face of the human I, it amounts to losing the human person." (p. 68)

e) To completing the arc of thought, "this I, this alienated I, is an I without God." An I without God, however, "cannot avoid boredom and nausea. So, we let ourselves go on living: we can feel ourselves part of a whole (pantheism), or else fall prey to desperation (the prevalence of evil: nihilism)." (p. 69)

Here, too, is it possible to reverse the trend? How can we avoid letting these "Five Withouts," like the three reductions described before, continue to empty out the life of faith and the possibility for a rich and fulfilled humanity? There is a single road: recovering Christianity in its true nature, as an event.

"So, the presence of Jesus Christ is an event – according to the perception given to us (quite persuasively!) by our charism. It is an event that we encounter in the present, in the now, in circumstances, [...] as emergence of the mystery of the Church, the mysterious Body of Christ." Giussani reiterates: "A supernatural reality is a human reality in which the Mystery of Christ is present, a natural reality in which the Mystery of Christ is present (natural in the sense that it shows itself and becomes specific in a human face). It is the Church that emerges close to me." He goes into detail, describing his own experience: "It emerged close to me in precise circumstances, with my father and my mother, and then when I joined the seminary, and then when I began to meet people who became attentive and friendly to me because I was saying certain things, and, in the end, I was somehow channeled into a companionship that made and makes the mystery of the Church immediate for me. It is therefore an emergence of the Body of Christ. It is the company we call vocational, that is, the company that involves because it generates and is generated by the experience in which the charism has touched me." (p. 36–7)

Evoking St Augustine – *In manibus nostris sunt codices, in oculis nostris facta*[8] – Giussani clarified the nature of the phenomenon that is the charism: "*In manibus nostris sunt codices*, the Gospels to be read, the Bible to be read... but we would not know how to read them without the other clause: *in oculis nostris facta.* The presence of Jesus is nourished, comforted, proved by the reading of the Gospels and the Bible, but it is assured, it becomes evident among us through a fact, through facts that are presences." Facts that take on a very specific weight for those to whom they happen, who are touched and won over by them. "In the whole life of everybody there is a fact that has meaning, a presence which has been an influence throughout life, a presence tending to influence the whole of life: it has enlightened the way of conceiving, of feeling, of acting. This is called an event. That into which we are introduced stays truly alive, comes true every day." All it brings must become more and more ours: "So, every day [...] we must become aware of the event as it happened to us, of the encounter we have had." (p. 37)

Only an experience of Christianity that is in full continuity with the faith at the very beginning is still capable of fascinating people, so much that those who come across the event of Christ, in the particular human features through which it is encountered, can be seized just as John and Andrew were two thousand years ago. Giussani is a shining witness of that possibility in the present, which he describes by saying, "Christ, this is the name that indicates and defines a reality I have encountered in my life. I have encountered: I heard of it when I was a child, as a boy, and so on. It is possible to grow up knowing the word Christ well, but for many people He is not encountered, He is not really experienced as being present. In my case Christ bumped into my life, my life bumped into Christ, precisely so that I should learn to understand that He is the central point of everything, of the whole of my life. Christ is the life of my life: in Him is summed up all that I would desire, all that I look for, all that I sacrifice, all that develops in me out of love for the persons with whom He has put me." (p. 37)

Every newness, every practical consequence springs forth from this: "Christ, life of my life, certainty of a good destiny, and companionship in everyday life, a familiar companionship that transforms things into good. This is His efficacy in my life. Then morality not only starts from here, but here the thread of morality is attached, fixed and saved." To show how morality is born out of belonging to Christ, Giussani references St Peter's, "Yes.": "St Peter did not take as the motive of his love for Christ the fact of having been forgiven his many defects, his many mistakes, his many betrayals. He did not list his own mistakes, but, when he found himself face to face with Christ after the resurrection, and when Christ asked him, 'Simon, do you love me?' he answered, 'Yes.' It is the relationship with His word, which is the most human and the most divine, which makes us embrace everything in our daily existence." (p. 38)

As it was for Peter, so, too for us, "the memory of Him has to be daily, the surge with which He becomes familiar has to be daily, the company with Him has to become glad, and the memory of Him has to leave us glad, in whatever circumstance, in whatever condition, for [...] in you, O Lord, the love the Mystery has for me is made flesh. A certainty of reaching my happy destiny and hope throughout the unfolding of my life." What a liberation and possibility to breathe freely! With it breaks in a measure without measure, leaving us dumbfounded and pushing Giussani to say, "'Yes, Lord, you know I love you.' I might have made mistakes and betrayed a thousand times in thirty days, but this still stands, it must stand! I think that this is not a presumption, but a surprising, inconceivable yet ineffable grace, as Michelangelo Buonarroti said, "But, Lord, what am I to do if to my eye / no more Your ineffable courtesy appears?" (p. 38)

Christian life is simple, and we need to be simple to be able to embrace it: "Christ, and our 'Yes' to Him: paradoxically I say, this is humanly the easiest aspect. I say this a bit presumptuously, and a bit enthusiastically: it is the easiest aspect, [...] of all the moral duty we have in the world. For Christ is the word that explains everything: Christ is a man who lived as everybody else two thousand years ago, but who, risen from the dead, invested by the power of the Mystery – in which by then He participated in His own nature – takes hold of us day after day, hour after hour, action after action." (p. 38)

It is a simplicity that allows us to call the Mystery "You," recognizing Him as a familiar presence in our daily life. "The totality of the presence of the Mystery and its claim on our lives ('God all in all') and of Christ, of Jesus of Nazareth, of the young man of Nazareth Jesus, who is the Mystery made Christ, His Christ, the totality of the one, of the great figure, of the enormous figure, of the enormous hint which God, which the word God is in our heart and on our lips, the totality of this familiar, daily, and efficacious presence of this companionship as strange as it is evidently insuperable. This totality explains our 'You.' To God we must say 'You,' and 'You, O Christ' we must say to the man Jesus of Nazareth." (p. 38)

What springs forth from the relationship with this incarnate You is the possibility of a new relationship that is more human – finally human – with everything: "You looked at all those to whom you spoke, or who answered You, or with whom there was no dialogue at all, even Pilate, even the Jewish high priests; the relationship You had with them was full, as it is proved by your passion, it was full of passion for their destiny, for the destiny of their persons, and your involvement with them presented you as being full of love for them. If they had welcomed, if they had come to agree with you, the word friendship would have been the only one they could have used for the relationship with You." The same is true today. "The word friendship is the only one we can use for our relationship with Him." (p. 39)

That incomparable presence made its way through history up to today, up to us, by means of a following, a continuity that was never interrupted: "The humanity of Jesus of Nazareth, which was called to participate in the mystery of divine nature, prolongs itself, so that the way that the Father has decided, in a sensible, visible, tangible reality – this people, which has an intelligent and affective appearance – may come about. It is the mystical Body of Christ, in other words, the tangible body of Christ in which the invisible divinity invests regions that the Father gives to the Son. This invasion generates men with a new mentality and a new fecundity." (p. 107)

Giussani underlines the historical and de facto conditions for this extension of Christ to reach us and to attract us: the charism: "The charism is an intervention of the Spirit of Christ in order to increase belonging to Christ in the world: it is a fact of the history in which we are born, in which the Spirit takes us by surprise, that history in which the Father has placed us. The plan of the originating Mystery, of the Father, has placed us on a given path, on a given road within the Church; it has immersed us in the fact of Christ, it has made us participate by making us His, in terms of our awareness and affection." The charism is a gift; it is "the charity that Christ has for us in making us His: His as awareness and affection, in other words, as mentality and as the way of dealing with and realising human affectivity." (p. 108)

Filled with this present Presence, at the end of the last Spiritual Exercises that he preached in 1999, Giussani addressed all those present saying this: "I want to leave you a wish. After all you have heard it might not be understood, but I do it all the same because there's nothing better I can say. [...] Through the grace of this encounter that we have been given, there is a potential in you that the Spirit has put there, implicitly or more explicitly, according to each one's own history, a capacity that the Spirit has put into you for witnessing to Christ, who is the only thing the world is waiting for, because where Christ is, relationships are peaceful, united and peaceful." Then he said, "My wish is that in this great thing, through this great thing that the Lord has given you, if it becomes more and more personal, that is to say, more obedient (because personalization, too, is obedience lived out intelligently), you may meet a father, you may have the experience of a father. [...] May each one of you discover the greatness of this role, which is not a role; it is the condition in which man looks at and sees God, and in which God entrusts to man what he most wants; father and therefore mother, because it's the same thing, spiritually they are not two different things; it is only materially that things change, when one has his own limitation and the other a different one. [...] May you live the experience of a father; father and mother; this is my wish for all the leaders, for all those responsible for your communities, but for each one of you, too, because each one has to be father to the friends he has around him, has to be mother of the people around about; not giving himself airs, but with real charity. For no-one could be as fortunate and glad as a man and a woman who feel they have been made fathers and mothers by the Lord. Fathers and mothers of all those they meet." (p. 119–20)

"Made fathers and mothers by the Lord." This is a longing we see growing inside of us, which extends to all those whom we meet, to all our human brothers and sisters who are, like us, wounded and full of an irreducible desire for happiness. The gratitude at having encountered a father who introduced us to the relationship with the Father just as Christ lived makes us desire to share the grace we have received with everyone, giving our lives for the work of Another.

Julián Carrón
September 2021

Editorial Note

Fr Luigi Giussani was tirelessly engaged in numerous educational initiatives throughout the course of his life. Much of his thought was, therefore, communicated through the richness and rhythm of oral discourse, and was handed on to us in that form (through audio and video recordings preserved in the Archive of the Fraternity of Communion and Liberation in Milan).

This volume has been compiled based on the transcriptions of a number of these recordings. The resulting text was edited in accordance with criteria formulated at the time of recording by Fr Giussani himself, described below:

1   Fidelity to speeches in the form in which they were spoken.
    The transcriptions were made with the aim of maximum
    adherence to the flow, the emphasis, and typical style of oral
    speech, as a concrete expression of the content and intentions
    of the author.

2   Respect for the nature of various speeches. Fr Giussani spoke
    in a range of diverse settings – conferences, university lectures,
    gatherings of CL leaders or other meetings, spiritual exercises,
    homilies, etc. – and was always careful to find the appropriate
    tone for each. In revising these interventions, the editors
    avoided standardizing or reorganizing content according to
    formal or structural criteria. Moreover, since his interlocutors
    were, whether explicitly or implicitly, a fundamental part
    of the crafting and expression of Giussani's thought, their
    interventions – in the context of dialogues or conversations –
    have typically been retained.

3 The passage from oral to written form is not to be considered
   as a transformation of the form of expression, but rather
   as the simple written rendering of a thought communicated
   orally. Where necessary, however, in order to avoid the
   awkwardness resulting from a mechanical transcription of the
   speech, the editors have eliminated mere repetitions of words
   or expressions, incidental circumstances not pertinent to the
   content, and superfluous interjections; and have corrected
   inconsistencies in syntax or grammatical agreement where it
   improves the readability of the text.

4 Where possible, references to people, events, or written
   works – whether implicit or explicit – have been clarified in
   the text or, alternatively, explained in a note or, after verify-
   ing the integrity of the meaning of the passage, been deleted.
   Explicit references to interlocutors present at the event or to
   public figures, where they are not essential for the development and comprehension of the subject matter, have generally
   been omitted.

The selection and editing of the texts in this volume was completed by Julián Carrón.

The volume contains texts that have already been published,
revised by Carmine Di Martino and Onorato Grassi, with editorial
coordination from Alberto Savorana.

TO GIVE ONE'S LIFE FOR THE WORK OF ANOTHER

You or About Friendship

(1997)

The words of Jean-Baptiste Massillon, "*Dieu seul est grand, mes frères* [God alone is great, my brothers]," spoken firmly and confidently without preamble, echoed in the great hall of the Rimini Fiera and set the tone for the year's Spiritual Exercises. Fr Giussani used them to introduce his reflection to the thousands of participants, before diving into the expansive theme of the Other in You or about Friendship. He was coming out of turbulent months that had weakened him, placing him in a human state that was unusual for him, burdened by illness and the effects of time. "Old age has erupted in me," he confided to a group of friends,[1] and his physical limitations regularly gave him pause to reflect on things that are passing, fading, ending. Instead of withdrawing or resigning himself, however, he reacted with a step toward renewal, going past appearances and committing his energies and his own intelligence to the search for a truth already known, but still to be discovered in its inner depths. It was a pensive time, full of intuitions, reflections, and critical analyses, to which he always tried to give a form and completeness, in that development of a discourse that had, perfectly, as one of its cornerstones his meditations for the Fraternity.

He went so far as to call the two lessons he gave for the Exercises that year, which explored man's self-awareness in relationship with the Great Presence, a kind of "real divine illumination," as the following pages can attest.

To a deepening of the content of the experience of faith, Giussani added a study of the modern and contemporary intellectual context and the mentality that flows from it, with which today's men and women must grapple, showing the deep connections between the two. Studying the history of humankind with the intention of demonstrating that life is ultimately positive was the invitation that Fr Giussani would later extend to his friends in the Fraternity in his final address at the Exercises in 2004. It was a task that he had taken on, and his incisive pages on modern rationalism, nihilism, and conceptions of I and human freedom offer the proof and testament of this.

For every speech and contribution, Fr Giussani prepared himself scrupulously. He wrote out notes, traced an outline, and documented sources by writing out quotes on index cards or sheets of paper. Then, he spoke, and in speaking created his discourse, almost on the spot, with a desire to communicate that captivated his listeners. Beginning with the 1997 Exercises, however, things changed. The fear that his physical limitations, including changes in his diction, could make it difficult to understand what he said led him to turn to a form of communication that was new to him, made available by technology. He preached the two principal meditations to a small group a few days before the larger gathering. They were recorded, and then were projected on large screens in the meeting rooms where the participants in the Exercises gathered together. The format did not change the substance, and the live experience was not diminished. Fr Giussani was present during the days in Rimini and watched the meditations in a small room backstage. On Sunday morning, he participated in the assembly, responding to questions spontaneously.

This new mode of communication turned out to be providential from that time on. In the months and years that followed, the use of video recordings and live remote connections allowed Fr Giussani to intervene in many gatherings of the movement and to closely follow the life of the movement, making up for the fact he could not be physically present. His "intrusions," as he called them, touched many souls and were the milestones of a journey that he passionately continued to travel along with his friends, even those "whom I do not know well, or whom I do not know at all, but with whom I feel a deep sense of togetherness."

———————

INTRODUCTION

"*Dieu seul est grand, mes frères*": God alone is great, my brothers. This is how the famous preacher Jean-Baptiste Massillon began the funeral speech for the Sun King.

The death of King Louis XIV of France was a signal of the epoch in which reason claimed to occupy the whole area of God's intervention in man, in every sense. Therefore, the Church, the ultimate source of light on man's experience, drew back its forces at the pastoral level in order to defend the people's morality – taking for granted that the dogmatic content was self-evident for a believer. Thus, the faith of God's people tended to lack defence and nourishment. It is through cultural work that a people's life consolidates and bears historical fruits, either for or against the Christian tradition that built up Western civilization.

It is as if we today were overwhelmed by the extreme consequences of the rationalistic rebellion against the living God who revealed Himself to man. "The living God.": Jesus calls Him this, because He is the God who has revealed Himself to man, the God who exists in history.

This is why we have to ask our Father who is in heaven to deepen the awareness of our faith: "who are You, Lord, for me, for us, for the whole world of men?" This is a step in which we hope in His help to conquer the dryness of our heart, so favoured by the common mentality.

I propose to attempt this by enlarging on what is taking up my thoughts these days, in two themes.

The first is this question: what is God for man? St Paul said, "God is all in all." (1 Cor 15:28). Who among us lives a continually revived awareness of this "God is all in all"? What does it mean?

And the second theme, how can we know Him as this? Jesus said: "No one knows who the Son is except the Father," (Lk 10:22). So I understand why in the Letter to the Colossians, ch.3, v.11, St Paul again repeats, "Christ is all and in all."

"GOD IS ALL IN ALL"

1. A New Beginning: Ontology

The theme of this first thought is St Paul's motto: "God is all in all."[2] Milosz in *Miguel Mañara* has the protagonist say, "Only He is."[3]

"For here we have no lasting city"[4] says the Letter to the Hebrews. This existence in me, or in human society, as it appears, with this ephemeral appearance that is yet full of presumption, in the unfolding of life produced by man in his dramatic social life, in the forms of his social being, is not a permanent existence, it is passing, it is ephemeral.

"When I see your heavens, the work of your fingers, the moon and stars that you set in place. What are humans that you are mindful of them, mere mortals that you care for them?"[5] says the Psalm. Yet we are that level of nature where nature lives in the awareness of itself, that vertiginous level in which reality, as it appears in its cosmic totality, has a paradoxical locus that contains it all in its potency, a point beyond our grasp, yet in which everything is mirrored: the I.

St Paul's sentence recalls a similar formula in the book of Sirach, "Now will I recall God's works; what I have seen, I will describe. At God's word were his works brought into being [...]. Perennial is his almighty wisdom; he is from all eternity one and the same, with nothing added, nothing taken away [...]. How beautiful are all his works! Even to the spark and the fleeting vision! [...] More than this we need not add; let the last word be, he is all in all!"[6]

Before this Lord the human I is thirsty for Him. The human I is thirsty for this God, that is, as Jesus says, "is thirsty for eternal life." Without this thirst everything would be opaque, obscure, an indigestible nothingness: the more one is a man, the more the I is aware and impulsively loving, the more everything would be stifling and intolerable without infinity. The I is thirsting for eternity, the I is relationship with infinity, that is, with a reality beyond every limit in which reality is known. He alone is: God, all in all.

"God is all." He is all precisely because of this thirst for infinity that defines the human phenomenon. That is, God is Being. Now, what does it mean that God is Being? Because He is all in all. He is everything. If God is Being because He is all in all, all that is, is made by God.

2. Two Temptations: Nihilism and Pantheism

But if God is all, what am I? What are you? What is the person I love? What is the fatherland? What is money? What are mountains and seas, flowers, and stars? What are the earth and the firmament?

The answer is not the solution of ethical concerns: it is the discovery of an ontology: the ontology of reality. But reality in its being, reality as it appears to our experience, that is, as it appears to man's reason, how is it there, and of what is it made? Reality as it appears to man is made by God, it is made "of" God. Being creates out of nothingness, that is, shares Himself. It is the perception that reality is contingent on the fact that reality is not self-made.

From the vertiginous perception of the ephemeral appearance of things, there develops, as a giving-in and as deceptive negation, the temptation of thinking that things are, or may be, illusion and nothingness. If God is all, then it means that the things you have, the people you live with, are either nothingness (nihilism), or are indistinct parts – as you also are an indistinct part – of Being, parts of God (pantheism). So, either pantheism or nihilism. These positions are today the ultimate answer to which everybody gives in, and which embraces us all when we lack a solid and clear standpoint.

Nihilism is the inevitable consequence, first of all, of an anthropocentric presumption, according to which man is capable, or would be capable, of saving himself. This is so false that all those who live defending this position, in the end, even openly, feel dissolved in a dualism whose bitterness they attempt to chase away in imagination, in imaginations borrowed from the Eastern world or from other kinds of movement, but in any case spiritualistic ones, of the Western world which always realize, at the end, a pantheistic ideal (as, for instance, the New Age from the United States).

An ideal that can be found even in Thomas Mann, in his *The Buddenbrooks,* when he describes the last man capable of defending the enormous, erudite wealth of the Buddenbrook family: a dramatic story that in him becomes tragic. In his day overburdened with work, in order to maintain the inheritance received from his father and grandfather, he can afford only ten or fifteen minutes of rest. "Lying in his armchair he rests" – Thomas Mann says – "thinking all the time of that ultimate instant when the drop that he is will be once again absorbed by the great sea," disappearing, as a drop, as individuality, plunging into the pacifying universal standardization.[7]

These two theories and attitudes (nihilism and pantheism) dictate all of today's behaviour; they are the only explanations of the common general mentality (also practical, or rather, above all practical); a general mentality which penetrates and weighs down everybody's head and heart, and therefore ours, too, Christian hearts, even many theologians' hearts. Both these theories, with all their consequences, play the same game, they have a common ground: the trust in power, and the longing for power however conceived, in any of its versions.

However conceived, in any version, power tends to be dictatorial; it is asserted as the only source, the only form of ephemeral, but possible order. The minimum of order, any need for order in a given social situation can have only power as its sure source. This, after all, was Luther's conception, which, in the end, leads to the absolute state: since all men are bad, it is better that there be only one who leads, or few people who lead. We could say that Lenin, Hitler, and Mussolini are identical from this point of view; but these, through a Calvinist Puritan mediation, are also identical with the democratic states, American or otherwise, and, apart from the form, they are identical with Yeltsin's Russia, or, perhaps we could say, with the present Italian government. In this culture, the state cannot be realized except as a cultural totalitarianism, unless it is attacked in its heart by something more Christian than the ideas and the practices on which it bases the whole of its wisdom.

How does one move from nihilism and pantheism to power as a target? If you ultimately reduce yourself to nothing, to a lie, to a pretence, if you feel you are a pretence, an appearance of being; if your I is born totally as a part of the great becoming, as appearance of being, as the mere outcome of its physical and biological forebears, you don't have an original consistency; the only criterion you can have is that of adapting yourself to what comes, just as it comes, to the mechanic impact of circumstances, and the more power you have in them, the more your consistency – which is appearance – increases, seems to increase, and therefore the illusion or rather, deception increases.

3. The Existence of the I

Both pantheism and nihilism destroy what is inexorably greatest in man, they destroy man as a person, that of whom Pascal says, the smallest thought is worth more than the whole of the universe, for it belongs to an infinitely greater reality. In fact, this is precisely Pascal's thought:

> All bodies, the firmament, the stars, the earth, and its kingdoms are not equal to the lowest mind; for mind knows all these and itself; and these bodies nothing. All bodies together, and all minds together, and all their products, are not equal to the least feeling of charity. This is of an order infinitely more exalted. From all bodies together, we cannot obtain one little thought; this is impossible, and of another order. From all bodies and minds, we cannot produce a feeling of true charity; this is impossible, and of another and supernatural order.[8]

The I is that level of reality in which what is real vibrates as a quest for relationship with infinity. It is called soul in traditional language, or spirit, a need for a totalizing relationship that transcends the precariousness of every possible relationship. Nihilism and pantheism destroy this I that defines the dignity of man, degrading it to the animal aspect, and the law of every gesture and every action is reduced to instinctivity: "My ravenous enemies are like lions eager for prey, like young lions lurking in ambush."[9]

Power, too, as a more dignified demonstration of the greater capacity man has above all other creatures, is exercised as possession, obtained through an instinct more cunning than that of the lion and the tiger, but identical in its dynamism: pride, violence, and sex (or "Usury, Lust, and Power,"[10] as Eliot said in the "*Choruses from 'The Rock'*").

So, to consider the answer to the question we have put: ("If God is all, what am I?"), how can the problem of man's being be solved? This is not only a philosophical problem, it is above all a problem of self-awareness, that is, a problem of the I, the person: what is at stake is what you are. This problem is at stake in every human gesture, in every experience when reality reveals itself to reason. But if you burn the content of experience by saying that you are nothing, or that you are an indistinct part of total being, then there is nothing outside you, you are the sole owner of yourself. Yet, if you are not the one with power, if you are not the boss, you are the slave of the power of others, whoever holds it: so, the child can be the slave of his father and mother, the woman of the man, the citizen of the state, or the region, the province or the municipal council; the more you belong to a small narrow society, the more you depend on those who hold the power in it.

Let us recall the question: "If He is all, what am I?" That is, if Being is God, what does it mean that I am? What does it mean that you are? The evident difficulty of this question leads to the immediate result that nihilism and pantheism appear to be the answer to reason as such, to reason not sufficiently informed. Nihilism, pantheism, and, ultimately, power. Any relationship becomes power, violence, and even the most tender relationship hides a hard wire inside. Except in children, perhaps; but, in adults, everybody.

To begin to look for the right answer, let us see what God says to Moses in the Bible. "You will tell them this: 'This is my name, I am, as the One who is, I am.'"[11]; "Only He is," (Milosz, in *Miguel Mañara,* had got it right) and this identifies God as Mystery. But, alongside this, even I myself "am," and this remains the only true mystery for reason; without this mystery reason does not reason, for reason is awareness of reality according to the totality of its factors. So nihilism and pantheism are a reduction, a negation of reason, a reductive simplification, contradictory to reason and they give in to the quantitative image of things: the quantitative image of being that comes to us from daily experience, from mortal life.

The only true mystery is therefore this: how is it that I am? Of what do I consist? Of what the thing before me consists? Of what do stones and the sea consist? This question identifies the ontological – not ethical – level of the question. On the contrary, nihilist and pantheist rationalism has exasperated precisely the ethical incidence of the question, reducing everything to the affirmation of man, and the affirmation of man is a *hybris,* it is a violence towards oneself, and the mystery of the world. The Church, too, attacked by rationalism, stressed ethics to the people and in her theology, taking ontology for granted and almost obliterating its originating force.

Having said all this, we cannot reasonably ignore the fact that for reason the Mystery must be – so to speak – reduced as much as possible. So how far can reason go; and therefore, where is the Mystery unassailable? Where is reason compelled to acknowledge the existence of an ultimate reality that it cannot penetrate? What in man can be conceived in some real way – though paradoxically – withdrawn from dependence on the God who creates it? Where does his being withdraw itself from being inevitably participant in Being (rather than a part of it)? Where can the I conceive itself independent

from the Being from which he derives? Where? In freedom! All the
rest can be challenged by reason, it is understandable by reason.
Because the fact that my hair does not make itself is evident to reason, that a flower does not make itself is evident to reason, that
I don't make myself is evident to reason. But how does the Mystery
who makes the flower operate, how does He make me?

More radically, how does the Mystery create something that is not
identified with Itself? This too is truly a mystery!

Everything, then, can be understood, except for one thing that is
still left out, and, according to reason, is still outside God: freedom.
Freedom is the only thing that appears to reason as being outside
God. Nothing can be added or taken away from Being as such.
Freedom, however, seems to take something away from the mystery
of Being, from God.

What is freedom? Let's start from experience as we usually do.
Freedom is the satisfaction of a desire. The phenomenon that makes
me say, "I am free" is a satisfaction. The phenomenon that defines
freedom is, therefore, the total satisfaction of me, the answer to
my thirst. Freedom is the need for a total satisfaction. This is why
it is adherence to Being. If Being, God is everything, freedom is to
acknowledge that God is all. The Mystery wanted to be recognized
by our freedom, It wanted to generate Its own recognition.

But in God Himself the acknowledgment is given by the Son, by
Him who was spoken to us as Word. For Jesus Christ God is Father,
and for the Father Jesus Christ is Son, therefore participant in the
Word, as the theology of the Most Blessed Trinity says. Thus in His
person, in His behaviour towards God, the Mystery is revealed as
Trinity. To accept love creates reciprocity, generates reciprocity. This,
in the Mystery, is nature. The nature of Being revealed itself in Jesus
of Nazareth as love in friendship, that is as love acknowledged. Thus
the mirror of the Father is the Son, the infinite Word, and in the
infinite mysterious perfection of this acknowledgment – in which
the infinite mysterious beauty of the origin of Being, of the Father
(*Splendor Patris*) vibrates for us – the mysterious creative power of
the Holy Spirit proceeds.

Now, the I, the human I made in the image and likeness of God,
originally reflects the Mystery of the one and triune Being, proper
to the dynamism of freedom, whose law will therefore be love, and
the dynamism in which this love is lived can be nothing else but
friendship.

There remains yet a point that is a mystery for my reason: why has God desired the participated being, in such a way that the participated being may not confine, may not tie Being within its boundary, may not rob anything from Being?

This is the heart of the Mystery: how the participated being does not rob anything from Being.

4. *Asking for Being*

So, as freedom, the nature of the participated being expresses itself – let us say that noble word immediately – as prayer.

If freedom is acknowledgment of Being as Mystery, the relationship between the participated being and God is only prayer. All the rest is done by God.

It is in prayer that the Mystery still persists, lasts as the ultimate explanation, it is in prayer and entreaty, for prayer is entreaty, entreaty to be. God wants there to be someone who asks to be, someone who says so sincerely that God is all, that he asks Him for what God has already given him, namely, to participate in Being.

If the created being is the participated being, freedom posits prayer as the only manifestation of the participated being: all that the participated being does is, in itself, prayer, that is, entreaty. Also in what he understands and perceives, the rational I worships the Mystery, finds himself before the Mystery. Not in front of but within the Mystery. If freedom is prayer and asking, it is within the Mystery.

Entreaty for what, then? Entreaty to be, to ask for Being, to ask for the Mystery. The nature of the participated being expresses itself as prayer, whose expression existentially is precisely entreaty, asking for Being. But what can it ask for? That being may become whole in him, in all that he does in existence, that is, in the amount of being that is communicated to him, of which he is constituted, in all that he does (for the being of the I is realized in action: "whether you eat or drink, whether you sleep or are awake, whether you live or die"[12]), to acknowledge that God is all, that all is made by God. *Omnis creatura Dei bona*: everything is good.[13] All is God. God is all.

From the positive point of view, God is all, and freedom is to acknowledge that God is all; from the passive point of view so to say, on the side of nothingness, all is God. This is Christian morality.

Christian morality coincides with this acknowledgment that really comes full circle where the Mystery becomes more of a mystery, unassailable even by man's imaginings, man's fantasy.

5. The Choice of Extraneousness

Sin is the contrary of truth and right, truth and good.

In every relationship, in any action, at any level of relationship, whichever relationship we live, sin is not acknowledging that God is all, as aim and method. In every relationship, sin is not living everything as an affirmation of God. Sin is not acknowledging God as origin, from whom the purpose and method of every action derive. "Only He is." So nothing is ours.

If this becomes an objection, it is due to a poison added by the father of lies: and the objection is self-idolatry.

As a matter of fact, in the Bible sin has an ultimate synonym: idolatry. The "father of all lies" (as Jesus will call the devil), works to spread the rational possibility of idolatry.

We can only say: sin is any action in which being able to say, "God is all" becomes an objection; any aspect that is not consistent with "God is all."

Thus man either tries to shy away, to hide before the presence of Being (as the first two at the beginning, Adam and Eve, did), or, in the end, gives himself up to despair: "They shall cry out to the mountains, 'Cover us!' and to the hills, 'Fall upon us!'"[14] on the last day.

Instead of God's familiarity that walks with Adam and Eve in the cool of the evening, we have the choice of extraneousness. Adam and Eve, rather than walking with God in the cool of the day, followed a stranger, something extraneous to their very experience. Extraneous: generated by the father of lies, Satan, whose only definition is "being against"; his freedom lived out as "being against." Not proving that God is not all, but being against the evidence that God is all. This is his nature, like the nature of every sin. Against the evidence, against what experience shows, Satan, like temptation, shows Being as a source of deception and of evil, and therefore as a deceptive vision. This is how the father of lies proves his falsity. Therefore, he emerges in human experience as something that is against the truth and good of man: as a "stranger," for Adam and Eve did not know it was the devil: under the appearance of a serpent he was a stranger, a stranger to their own experience.

When man rebels, he adheres to a reality that is extraneous to his being, adheres to "the world," as Jesus says, that is, the sum of power, which has an everyday shape (like the serpent to Adam and Eve, that of an animal), but inside it is not what it says it is, inside it is not what it shows itself to be, inside "it is not." Even Satan is a being participated by God, and therefore of God; not accepting this, not acknowledging this, is what makes Satan, and therefore the sinner, unhappy.

This explains, on the one hand, why whoever walks within this morality, a morality conceived as the acknowledgment that God is all, is glad; we find gladness, or anyway peace, even in the saddest situations. On the other hand, whoever follows, whoever gives in to the father of lies, the devil, who does not acknowledge that God is all (though he is made of Him), whoever gives in to a stranger is the victim, the slave and the victim, of a principle that hates him, that does not love him, which is the world: he becomes the slave of the world. And the more successful his career, the more this slavery becomes patent. St Ambrose said, "See how many masters have those who do not want to have the only Lord."[15]

"CHRIST IS ALL AND IN ALL"

1. Nature and Destiny of the Person

"Christ is all and in all."[16] This sentence of St Paul's is worthy of the citation that Maximus the Confessor makes in his *Mystagogia*: "Christ," he says "is [...] all in all of us. He who embraces everything in Himself according to the unique, infinite, and most wise power of his bounty, as a centre into which all lines converge, so that the creatures of the one God may not remain strangers and enemies to each other, but have a common locus where they can manifest their friendship and their peace."[17] It sums up the roots of all that we think and feel in our clear conviction of faith.

First of all, St Paul's sentence. If "God is all in all," what does it mean that "Christ is all and in all"? Theology often tries to equate these two statements by replacing "all" with "everybody" in the first one. But the first Letter to the Corinthians 15:28 says: "When everything is subjected to him, then the Son himself will (also) be subjected to the one who subjected everything to him, so that God may be all in all [ìna é ò theòs pànta en pàsin]."[18] The Greek *en pàsin* can be either masculine or neutral. Yet in this case, in the context of St Paul's formulation, they can only be translated in the neutral: "Everything will have been subjected to Him, [...] He subjected everything to Him" so that "God be all (*pànta*) in all (*en pàsin*)." God all in all is not only a possible, but the necessary version, given the ultimate and more comprehensive context of the formulation.

In the Letter to the Colossians 3:11, there is the other formulation: "There is not Greek and Jew, circumcision and uncircumcision, barbarian, Scythian, slave, free, but Christ is all and in all [*allà tà pànta kaì en pàsin Chrìstos*]." Here *en pàsin* is masculine plural, the context gives it both motive and stress, and therefore the correct translation is: "All and in all [in everyone]." The difference between the two has an essential meaning.

First of all, "Christ is all and in all" is, in its ontological value, the link between the mystery of the person of Christ and the nature and destiny of the person of each man: this is the real, ontological value of "Christ is all and in all." This is why Jesus says at the Last Supper in his last speech before his death, turning to the Father, "You have given me power over every human being [literally: "over all flesh"] so that I may give eternal life to all those You have given me."[19]

But, secondly, "Christ all in everyone" means that, not only ontologically, but also for man's self-awareness, Christ is the original source, the ultimate and adequate example that makes it possible for man to conceive and live his relationship with God (the Creator) and his relationship with the other man (a creature), and his relationship with the cosmos, with history and society.

2. The Imitation of Christ

Why is the relationship with God a relationship with Jesus? Because Jesus is the unveiling, the revealing of God as Mystery, of the Trinity as Mystery. Thus "morality" is for man the imitation of Jesus Christ's behaviour, the behaviour of the man Jesus, of Jesus Man-God, a man in whom God is.

He is for everybody the Master (*"Magister adest."* [The Master is here.];[20] "Don't call yourselves masters. Only one is your Master."[21]), the Master to be discovered, listened to, and followed. "Blessed are those who listen to the Word of God and put it into practice in their lives."[22] The imitation of Christ is knowledge of the truth, the practice of the truth for everybody.

Jesus Christ goes on in history, in all times, within the Mystery of the Church, His Body, made up of all those the Father has given into His hands, as He Himself says, and whom He, by the power of His Spirit, has identified with Himself as members of His Body through baptism. The magisterium of Christ is, and therefore coincides with, that of the Church, for by her it is authentically read and heard.

At this point allow me an observation. What we said before about power applies in a vertiginous way to authority as it might be lived in the Church. If it is not fatherly, and therefore motherly, it can become a source of supreme misunderstanding, the most subtle and destructive tool in the hands of falsehood, of Satan, the father of lies.[23] Whereas in the end, in an unsettling way, the authority of the Church paradoxically must always be obeyed.

From the institutional point of view, it is to be obeyed because what it says is the instrument and the carrier of tradition, in as much, that is, as it is formally orthodox in faith and obedient in practice to the authority of the Pope. So, from the institutional point of view, the authority is the contingent form that the presence of the risen Jesus makes use of as the operative expression of his friendship with man, with me, with you, with each one of us. This is the most striking aspect of the mystery of the Church, which most affects man's self-respect, man's very reason.

The meaning of the imitation of Christ, of imitating Christ, then, is authentically indicated by the Church's moral teaching for all men, but initially and first of all for the baptized, the faithful. The Church is therefore the source with which the whole of morality is to be compared, the defining of life's morality as awareness of man's duty and his tending to carry it out, in the light of Christ's own awareness, the only Master of mankind (*Unus est enim Magister vester*).[24] In baptism – the fundamental gesture by which in the life of the Church a man is made immanent in the Mystery of Christ – the "new creature" is born.[25] This is the new ontology, the new being, the new unimaginable participation in Being, in Being as Mystery; it is from here that the new morality derives.

But how is it possible to imitate Christ, the man Jesus of Nazareth, in the infinite diversity of the mysterious identity of each man who believes in Him? What a mysterious identity lives in each man who believes in Him!

Jesus is the man whom the Spirit of God – as for any man – caused to be born of a woman, to live and to die as the son of a mother, whose I, whose personality was invested and identified with the very nature of the Mystery, so that what it is possible to know of the Mystery was revealed immediately by Him.

Thus, we came to know that the man Jesus is made immanent in the Word of God, Son of the Father. Hence, the imitation of Christ is possible if man acknowledges himself as "the adoptive son" of God as Father, as mysteriously participant in God's nature, chosen by Jesus, Man-God, to be part of Him in the baptismal mystery, made a member of His Body.

For all these reasons the Church makes use of the definition "adoptive son," aroused by the Spirit of Jesus to call "adoptive" our sonship. "But when the fullness of time had come, God sent his Son, born of a woman, born under the law, to ransom those under the law, so that we might receive adoption. As proof that you are children, God sent the spirit of his Son into our hearts, crying out, 'Abba, Father!' So, you are no longer a slave but a child, and if a child then also an heir, through God."[26] This is why the Apocalypse at the end says: "The victor [he who will follow Christ on the Cross, on that Cross that lifts Him up to His resurrection and to His Lordship over the whole world], will inherit these gifts, and I shall be his God, and he will be my son."[27] Here he is speaking of man, the man who is called and faithful to his call.[28]

But if morality for man is to imitate Christ, let us ask ourselves: how does Christ behave towards the Father, how does Christ behave towards man as neighbour, towards the other created by the Father, towards society and therefore history, the whole history of mankind?

3. God is Father

First of all, the behaviour of Jesus, of the Man-God towards God is marked by the acknowledgment that God, the Mystery, is paternity. In Jesus' awareness there lives the totality of the Father's intrusiveness, the intrusiveness of the "God who is all in all."

> Amen, amen, I say to you, a son cannot do anything on his own, but only what he sees his father doing; for what he does, his son will do also. For the Father loves his Son and shows him everything that he himself does, and he will show him greater works than these, so that you may be amazed.[29]

Jesus introduces man to the acknowledgment of this paternity, of this supreme familiarity with the Mystery that constitutes him, that makes all things. "In praying," Jesus says "do not babble like the pagans, who think that they will be heard because of their many words. Do not be like them. Your Father knows what you need before you ask him. This is how you are to pray: Our Father who art in heaven… [that is, in the depth, in the generative root of things.][30]

Jesus said of Himself, "I am the way and the truth and the life. No one comes to the Father except through me. If you know me, then you will also know my Father. From now on you do know him and have seen him." Philip said to him, "Master, show us the Father, and that will be enough for us." Jesus said to him, "Have I been with you for so long a time and you still do not know me, Philip? Whoever has seen me has seen the Father."[31]

The only Lord, the Mystery that makes all things and all time in which things exist, and subsist, becomes familiar to us through Jesus (the man chosen by Him and made part, immediately participant in His divine nature, in the nature of the Mystery itself). In this man we see the defining of what humanly speaking it would be a presumption to define (it could be the expression of an utmost desire, of the original longing of our awareness, but how uncertain, how rare and uncertain, and full of mistaken motives are the erratic ways of man's thought!): God is Father, the Mystery is fatherly. What is more familiar than this radical positivity, this good of which as human experience the father is the source?

4. Jesus' Behaviour towards the Father

How, then, does Jesus behave towards the Father? If He reveals to us first of all that God is Father, the Mystery is Father, how does his behaviour unfold?

a) Of this Father, of this Mystery as Father, Jesus stresses the creative power: this is the behaviour towards a father who is the Creator. Of a human existence which is a journey towards a perfection, of a human life which is weakness, fragility, inconsistency, and vertigo; of all of this, even of all of this, even of His creature who is in these conditions, He is the Redeemer, He redeems.

Christ addresses the Father as Creator.

He is the first man with an adequate and perfect awareness that all his content as man is the presence of the Father. Meditating on some chapters of St John's Gospel (like chapters 5, 6, 7, 8) we can trace a dominant thought in Christ's words: He does what the Father wants, He sees the Father, He does nothing but what He sees the Father is doing. When He watched the sparrow fall, when He observed the lilies in the field, the harvest, a man's hair, what gave Him the certainty of drawing hints from everything to reach the meaning of the world, the meaning of his own life? What made this certainty flourish was His relationship with the Father, the Father's company.[32]

For us to imitate Jesus, therefore, is to live first of all religiosity in every gesture. This first aspect, this first article of morality is clear to us: to live religiosity in every gesture. St Paul says it several times: "Whether we are awake or asleep we may live together with him.";[33] "Whether you eat or drink, or whatever you do, do everything for the glory of God,"[34] or for Christ's glory, because God communicates to us in Jesus' word and in His person.

This is why the dynamic law of existence for Christ is obedience (to live everything for the reasons of Another); for us, this finds its utmost expression in offering. Offering is the acknowledgment that, like God, Christ is the *substantia* of the whole of life, that is, He is the consistency and the meaning, the value of the relationship between man and any reality in life. The value of the relationship between man and any reality in life is Christ; whatever relationship is involved. The meaning is Christ; therefore, obedience, offering is to live for the reasons which are directed to the word Christ, as Christ lives for the reasons of the Father. Hence the religiosity of every gesture, every action, every relationship.

b) Secondly, Jesus' behaviour towards God the Father as supreme perfection, and therefore life as continual tension towards Him: "Be perfect, just as your heavenly Father is perfect."[35] The meaning of man's existence is a journey of perfection. The aim of existence is that the creature may live life as much as possible as a tension towards the perfection of the Mystery.

Morality is lived thus, not as definition of a measure or of laws, but as the tension to an imitation of Christ and its consequences. "Until heaven and earth pass away, not the smallest letter or the smallest part of a letter will pass from the law.";[36] "Don't think that

I have come to abolish the law or the prophets, I have not come to abolish, but to fulfill,"[37] that is, in this tension, to make it possible. "Everyone who has this hope based on Him makes himself pure, as He is pure."[38] Making morality possible as a continuous tending to imitate Christ in His obedience to the Father.

In what sense, then, did Christ "not come to abolish, but to accomplish," that is, to make it possible? The tension is like the ultimate and permanent expression of freedom before the "God who is all in all." That this tension becomes consistency in man is grace. So, the thread of morality is a sincere entreaty for this grace. Sincere entreaty is the fundamental form of prayer: it is begging. Like in the prayer of the tax collector:

> Two people went up to the temple area to pray; one was a Pharisee and the other was a tax collector. The Pharisee took up his position and spoke this prayer to himself, 'O God, I thank you that I am not like the rest of humanity – greedy, dishonest, adulterous – or even like this tax collector. I fast twice a week, and I pay tithes on my whole income.' But the tax collector stood off at a distance and would not even dare to raise his eyes to heaven but beat his breast and prayed, 'O God, be merciful to me a sinner.' I tell you, the latter went home justified; not the former; for everyone who exalts himself will be humbled, and the one who humbles himself will be exalted.[39]

Whoever says: "I can"; "I have the power"; "I have the strength," will find it proved that he can get the strength, not from himself but only through Another to whom he asks that he can have all that.

In morality, then, what has to prevail is entreaty and begging rather than the fulfilment of a resolution: it would be a presumption, not a resolution, if it weren't entreaty. What a great truth this parable in the Gospel re-proposes to us!

c) Lastly, let us see Jesus' behaviour towards God the Father as Redeemer, and therefore as *mercy*.

"For God so loved the world that He gave His only Son, so that everyone who believes in Him might not perish but might have eternal life."[40] So the meaning of this Son, of this Word made flesh, identified with a man born of woman, is to reveal completely the love of the Mystery, the love the Mystery has for His creature: to reveal fully the love of God the Father.

Christ, this man born in Bethlehem, who lived in Nazareth, in that precise and fleeting moment of history, is our destiny-made presence and companionship, He is the Mystery of God made into presence and lasting companionship, for the whole time of His creature. "I am with you always, until the end of the age,"[41] the supreme affirmation of the Creator as love.

In Jesus God's relationship with His creature is revealed as love, and therefore as mercy.

What does the word mercy add to the word love or forgiveness? To the word love nothing can be added, but to our perception of the meaning of this word, the word mercy adds something: it adds the factor of the Mystery, so that all our measures and imaginations fail. Mercy is the attitude of the Mystery, it shows the attitude of the Mystery before any human weakness, mistake, or forgetfulness: God loves man whatever crime he commits.

The acceptance of this mercy, the acknowledgment of this mercy is the high point of morality, the summit of morality; this acceptance is the depth of the authenticity of the acknowledgment that man has, that man's freedom realizes of the Mystery as the source of everything, of the "God is all in all."

We cannot beg of God the Father except as a surrender to His mercy.

5. From Friendship to Morality

In brief, Christ's behaviour towards God the Father is the acknowledgment or acceptance of the Mystery as mercy. Therefore, the relationship between Jesus and the Father constitutes the supreme actualization of friendship.

Jesus as a man acknowledges and accepts to be, Himself, His Father's mercy. Thus He accepts to die: "Father, forgive them, they know not what they do."[42]

Just as obedience to the Father represents the source and the summit of virtue for the man Jesus, so for man morality is born as a prevalent, irresistible liking for a person who is present: Jesus. In spite of everything – attractiveness, sorrow, and crime – the attachment to Jesus prevails. Man's morality is born, then, as friendship with God as Mystery and, therefore, with Jesus, through whom and in whom the Mystery unveils, reveals and communicates Himself.

Through friendship is every relationship in which the other's need is shared in its ultimate meaning, that is in that destiny for which and to which every need awakens and expresses man's thirst and hunger. For men to accept this love – that is expressed in the will of God, in the will of the Mystery who, by becoming a man, accepts death, his death for all His sons – this is the beginning of morality, that is born as friendship with God. As for Jesus morality comes from accepting to be the very subject of the mercy of the Father – He accepts this Mystery that is communicated to Him, He accepts it by dying for men – thus for man, for every man, morality is born as friendship with Him, with God in Him, in Jesus.

Morality is born as friendship with God as Mystery and therefore with Jesus. Man's relationship with God as Mystery and therefore with Jesus starts and accomplishes all its greatness, its simplicity, its truth, its security, in St Peter's "Yes" to Jesus who asked him, "Simon, do you love me?"

Through Peter's "Yes" morality is the surprise of a Presence to which we adhere in such a way that the whole of life tends to be conceived through it, in its details and in its globality, so that it may please the face of that Presence. Therefore, morality for a Christian is loving adherence.

6. Light, Strength, and Help

Let us now look in detail at how Jesus behaves towards the other, towards man as neighbour.

Synthetically, it means sharing man's life as a source of light, strength, and help. A sharing in man's life as a source of light, strength, clarity, truth, energy, and help.

a) As a source of *light*: "The true light, which enlightens everyone, was coming into the world."[43] Or, as He was to say at the Last Supper, "I revealed your name to those whom you gave me out of the world. They belonged to you, and you gave them to me, and they have kept your word. Now they know that everything you gave me is from you, because the words you gave to me I have given to them."[44]

So, for us, for the man He chooses, the values through which to judge are those that pay attention to the word of the Word as

presence of Jesus: as Presence now. But this is the community of
the Church to which we belong, the face of this Presence, or that in
which the face of this presence becomes perceivable, becomes sign, a
sign, though, that contains that of which it is a sign. The community
of the Church is the locus where the event of Christ's presence is
renewed, is new, is born.

The method the Mystery has used to give Himself, to reveal Himself
to His creature is the sacramental method: a *sign* that contains the
Mystery of which it is the sign. The community of the Church is
the aspect of this sign, is the visible aspect of that face. It is the clothing of that Presence, as the clothes of Jesus for the little children who
stayed close to Him. The very small children, four to five years old,
who surrounded Jesus and grabbed hold of His legs, sticking their
noses into his clothes, and didn't see his face, they didn't remember his
face, perhaps didn't even look at it. But they were there with Him. So
that the clothes, the seamless tunic in which Jesus was clad, were fixed
in their eyes more than His face. Similarly, Jesus makes Himself perceivable to us in the ecclesial community, as if it were the clothing with
which our smallness enters into relationship with His real presence.

Listening to the voice of the authority, that is of the Pope and of
the official acts of the Church, is like the antidote to drinking in the
slogans of the mass media.

"Do not conform yourselves to this age but be transformed by the
renewal of your mind, that you may discern what is the will of God,
what is good and pleasing and perfect."[45] It was Josef Zvěřina,[46] a
great man of the Czechoslovakia of some decades ago, persecuted
for his faith, who, in his "Letter to the Christians of the West,"[47]
quoted to us this passage from St Paul's Letter to the Romans.

The judgment that decides over the act and over the human
day is knowledge of the truth, through the Church as presence of
the Truth. Not the Church of the Theologians, but the Church of the
Sacraments, of the Pope's word and that of the bishops in as much as
they are united to him, the Church of those who acknowledge in the
humility and the suffering of the great anticipation (that conquers
suffering in the gladness of hope), the word of the Pope and of the
bishops who guide this reality of true Church.

Perhaps in some moments of Jesus' life, some pious woman or
some humanly mature and sensitive disciple will have said, "Poor
Jesus!" It is an analogy by which we can say – but with the same
pity, for the same reason and the same causes: "Poor Church!" Not

as a negative judgment, but as a sad observation, though full of the certainty of resurrection in the life of the Church today.

b) Jesus as a source of *strength*. "Without me you can do nothing."[48] I wonder how the apostles during the Last Supper, in that last supper, in that dreadful evening full of trembling and terror, listened to that sentence: "Without me you can do nothing"! Therefore, we are beggars, and the form of begging enlightened by Christ are the sacraments. For sacrament, as it is the supreme form of prayer, "must also be a plea to God, emerging from the tiniest aperture of desire for liberation."[49]

c) Lastly, as a source of *help*. "I am among you as the one who serves."[50] "The Son of Man did not come to be served but to serve and to give his life as a ransom for many."[51] He becomes the servant of everybody precisely because He gives man the energy for the journey towards his destiny, that is towards Him.

Thus, all the relationships with man in Jesus are a sharing. There is no true relationship except in function of destiny: for it is towards destiny that every human need tends, every need of the participated being which is called man. When man lives this, accepts this, seeks in every relationship the destiny of the other, then all relationships are good, and in every relationship man accepts the help that comes to him from the Mystery through the other, however much or little it be, because through the other the Mystery helps man, much or little, when man lives relationships – the relationship with his companion, with the other – with the awareness of his destiny.

Thus, in any relationship we start with a positive hypothesis. The secret soul of each relationship is friendship: to want the other's destiny, to accept that the other wants my destiny. If I acknowledge and accept that the other acts for my destiny, then this is friendship.

Christian friendship is brotherly friendship, the most familiar friendship. St Bernard described it in a wonderful way:

Charity [says St Bernard] generates friendship, it is like its mother [charity is love for the other as affirmation of his good destiny, as a desire to affirm that his right destiny should be fulfilled, for Christ is the Mystery of which He is a part, and in which He participates]. It is God's gift, it comes from Him, for we are carnal. He causes our desire and our love to begin from the flesh. In our hearts God inscribes for our friends a love that they cannot read, but that we can show to them. The outcome is an affection, more often an *affectus*, a profound, inexpressible attachment, which is in the order of experience and which fixes rights and duties for friendship.[52]

This is the friendship of St Peter, Simon the son of John, with Jesus, when he still did not know, he had not realized, he had not fully appreciated what Jesus ultimately wanted to say of Himself.

"It is charity that generates friendship, it is like its mother." Charity, that is the relationship in which the other's destiny is sought with the awareness of a person who has been called by it, in the certainty of the consciousness that the other's destiny is Jesus, the God-made man, since through that man God enters into relationship with us.

7. Within the World History: Ecumenism and Peace

Lastly, the behaviour of Jesus towards society, precisely as an institution.

a) First of all, let us see how He behaved towards the institution, the institutional locus which is called state, nation, or, even better, fatherland, originally people, the people in that fatherland. On this point of view there are impressive quotations:

"I was sent only to the lost sheep of the house of Israel."[53] The value of the fatherland, or of society which a people expresses, in its characteristics, and also in its limits, is here underlined. But this love for the fatherland has a destiny of usefulness for the whole world. "The forgiveness of sins, would be preached in his name to all the nations, beginning from Jerusalem."[54]

One evening He sees his city from the hill and He weeps, thinking of her ruin:

> Jerusalem, Jerusalem, you who kill the prophets and stone those sent to you, how many times I yearned to gather your children together as a hen gathers her brood under her wings, but you were unwilling! Behold, your house will be abandoned. [But] I tell you, you will not see me until [the time comes when] you say, "Blessed is he who comes in the name of the Lord."[55]

Weeks later that city would kill Him, but for Him this doesn't matter. Or that other night, immediately before He was taken, in the golden splendor of the temple illuminated by the setting sun, *edákruse*, the Greek text says, He sobbed in front of His city's destiny. It is pity like that of a mother who clings to her child so he does not fall into the mortal danger he's headed for.[56]

Love for the fatherland is a profound implication of Christian *pietas*, but only in as much as the fatherland is in function of earthly welfare and of the eternal good of the whole of mankind.

b) Secondly, the attitude of Jesus towards society as political power, political power, both Roman and Jewish, of his time:

> So Pilate went back into the praetorium and summoned Jesus and said to him, "Are you the King of the Jews?" Jesus answered, "Do you say this on your own or have others told you about me?" Pilate answered, "I am not a Jew, am I? Your own nation and the chief priests handed you over to me. What have you done?" Jesus answered, "My kingdom does not belong to this world. If my kingdom did belong to this world, my attendants (would) be fighting to keep me from being handed over to the Jews. But as it is, my kingdom is not here." So, Pilate said to him, "Then you are a king?" Jesus answered, "You say I am a king. For this I was born and for this I came into the world, to testify to the truth. Everyone who belongs to the truth listens to my voice." [...] Pilate [...] went back into the praetorium and said to Jesus, "Where are you from?" Jesus did not answer him. So, Pilate said to him, "Do you not speak to me? Do you not know that I have power to release you and I have power to crucify you? [...] Jesus answered (him), "You would have no power over me if it had not been given to you from above. For this reason the one who handed me over to you has the greater sin." [A sin greater than yours.]"[57]

Political power, too, draws its possible earthly positivity only if it is in function of a universe, of everybody, of everyone in the world. Otherwise, "the one who handed me over to you has the greater sin."

This other passage of John tells us about His relationship with the Jewish power:

> But one of them, Caiaphas, who was high priest that year, said to them, "You know nothing, nor do you consider that it is better

for you that one man should die instead of the people, so that the whole nation may not perish." He did not say this on his own, but since he was high priest for that year, he prophesied that Jesus was going to die for the nation, and not only for the nation, but also to gather into one the dispersed children of God.[58]

c) Lastly, Jesus' attitude towards history.
We must imitate Jesus in his behaviour towards history, because the human glory of Christ is acknowledged by us as the meaning of history, of our own personal existence and of its total context, which is called history. "Father, the hour has come. Give glory to Your Son, so that Your Son may glorify You, just as You gave Him authority over all people, so that He may give eternal life to all You gave Him."[59] As for Jesus the meaning of history was the fulfilment of the Father's will ("This is eternal life, that they should know you, the only true God, and the one whom you sent, Jesus Christ"),[60] so for man the imitation of Christ is to live every day the aim of every action as the affirmation of the meaning of history, which is Jesus Christ Himself: Christ's human glory.

Witnessing is living for Christ's glory. It is the phenomenon by which men acknowledge – by a powerful grace, by a powerful gift – of what reality is made, of what things themselves are made: it is made of Christ, and they shout it to everybody; they prove it by their own existence, by the transformed mode of their own existence as presence. The end of history will be the day in which the whole human universe will be compelled to acknowledge this.[61]

Every time in history, every measure of time deserves, that is, matches eternity, in so far as it lives the memory of Christ. Therefore, Christian morality implies that social, cultural, political commitment be educated, and so mature in the concrete ideal of a reminder of and a help in keeping the memory of Christ, and therefore the sense of history as the meaning of time and of relationships.

A morality that does not make us live every gesture, – from washing dishes to being in parliament, – in its cosmic dimension of offering to Christ cannot be a Christian morality. Offering is to acknowledge that the *substantia*, the consistency of the being that lives, that is lived in a relationship, that is expressed in a relationship, is Christ: an acknowledgment that cannot but be sustained by the prayer that He may be visible, may show and prove Himself.

So, human social life lives as its ideal what is expressed in the Letter to the Hebrews: "Exhort one another every day, as long as 'today' lasts, that none of you may be hardened by the seduction of sin. Exhort one another every day: recall the memory of Christ every day, remind each other of the memory of Christ. Since it is for this that we have become sharers of Christ: on condition that we keep firm to the end the trust we have had at the beginning."[62]

Hence the obedience that safeguards order in society. But what really safeguards order in society is authority: "Let every person be subordinate to the higher authorities, for there is no authority except from God, and those that exist have been established by God. [...] For rulers are not a cause of fear to good conduct."[63]; "Be subject to every human institution for the Lord's sake."[64] What man lives cannot be in contradiction with this.

Hence the commitment to serve the human community in culture, economy, politics, according to all the capacity of our gratuitousness, therefore of our free time, too, but first in our work.

Ecumenism and peace are the outcome favoured in all this. In them the actualization of a friendship tendentially universal, where human history finds its best support is affirmed, as the principle of every relationship, as the supreme contribution of every social reality.

This means that Christian friendship takes part in the generation of the social reality, of the social reality as a people. That is, from the actualization of this friendship a people is born, for only in reciprocity does a man become a father, acquire a paternity, that is, generate. Fatherhood is the level where nature is self-aware, it is the human level. The animal is generator-reproducer, not father. The father is the supreme help in clarifying the meaning of life and companionship on life's journey.

Any relationship, provided it is realized in reciprocal love, that is friendship, generates something human. This is our contribution, the contribution of the Church's morality to peace both here and everywhere. On the contrary, what the world contributes in relationships is called violence, at every level, even in the most hidden formations, the ones most cunningly underhand, cunningly and unconsciously underhand many times, except for sudden leaps in the original fulcrum, in the original nature: father, mother and child. The leaps of mankind, however, are reduced to jerks without great power, which can do nothing on the river, on the all-sweeping worldly tide, and are therefore reduced to powerless jerks against violence, against the *hỳbris* that inevitably intervenes when God becomes extraneous, extraneous to the conception, the making of the relationship.

On the contrary, from the event of Christian friendship lived as ecumenism and peace a people is born: it is a conception of life, a way of feeling what is real, an honesty before the circumstances, an intense answer to a provocation according to a vision, a perception of our destiny of truth and happiness. And there is not only the individual who grows up, gets married and two, or six, children are born. Imagine the hundreds of nuns of Hildegard of Bingen, and, at the same time, the monks of Peter the Venerable, in Cluny, and all the people who flocked there. This is the way in which, slowly, from the barbarity that dominated the 5th and 6th centuries, the Christian family came out, with its typical tenderness of sentiments, the capillarity of attentions, the clarity of commands and laws; "the Christian family as organism and as home, the true home for man: help, shelter, hospitality, song."[65]

To identify the ideals gathered in the word ecumenism and in the word peace with an earthly power contradicts all of this. Power transforms these ideals, these very ideals, into violence: ecumenism becomes the affirmation of one's position, closed and violent, or an intemperate denial of every meaning, every relevance, every esteem; and peace becomes a formula made into a password for winning your own war.

Violence always implies the attempt to destroy a people, at all times: the violence of armies, of magistrates, or even of the religious realities in which religiosity does not find an open adherence and real consequentiality.

All the education imparted by power drives man, the family, the conception of social life, the way of relating with others to violence, which is the method of relationship with others. Power endorses all forms of ultimate strangeness, which are the beginning of this violence in the world.

On the contrary, no presence is a stranger to the man who follows Christ. So, "If you are what you ought to be, you will set fire to all Italy.";[66] "Do not be satisfied with little things, because God wants great things!";[67] thus St Catherine, the illiterate young woman from Siena, wrote.

But the Mystery as mercy remains the last word, even on all the ugly possibilities of history. The Mystery as mercy. This is the most irresistible embrace, in its evident compassion, of Being, the source of Being, the aim of Being, the nature of Being; it is the whole relationship of Being with my nothingness, with me, which He made, and which he granted to participate in Him. This is the ultimate embrace of the Mystery, against which man – even the man who is most distant, most perverse, most darkened and loving of darkness – can oppose nothing, can raise no objection: he can desert Him, but in this case he would be deserting himself and his own good. The Mystery as mercy remains the ultimate word even on all the ugly possibilities of history.

ASSEMBLY

STEFANO ALBERTO (FR PINO): For that young woman the beginning of every day, the beginning of every gesture, every action was marked, penetrated by, and full of the awareness of that Presence, of the human presence of that child, and later of that man: a companionship of the Mystery accompanying Mary's destiny, the Mystery's human companionship for us on our journeying.

Angelus[68]

Morning prayer[69]

GIANCARLO CESANA: We received hundreds of questions, as is traditional by now. The questions show one thing: that we were faced with a new proposal, an unexpected one too, on which we must work and reflect. This should come as no surprise because the Exercises train us to reach our objective which is life. They introduce us to the great journey of life.

I will now ask Fr Pino some questions concerning points that were repeatedly asked during the assemblies, and then I will pose two fundamental questions to Fr Giussani.

First question (the questions addressed to Fr Pino concern especially the theme of freedom): "Could you go back over the issue of freedom, and explain what is meant by 'freedom is the only point that cannot be attacked by reason'?"

FR PINO: "The only point that cannot be attacked by reason" means above all that it is the only point where the Mystery remains mystery, totally mystery, because – Fr Giussani stressed this passage in his lesson – the fact that things are not self-made is evident to reason, that I in this moment am not making myself is evident to reason. Reason does not understand how this happens, it cannot understand how, but that things in this instant are from Another, this is evident.

But there is a point which reason really cannot attack: reason cannot understand precisely the fact of freedom as a possibility to acknowledge the Mystery or not. It is in this point that the Mystery remains unassailable.

LUIGI GIUSSANI: Nothing can be added to Being as such, or taken from it: but freedom seems to take away something from the Mystery of being, from God, because freedom brings also a possibility that the creature, the participated being, becomes the devil, falsehood, denying the aspect of receiving. Freedom is the possibility that the participated being sets itself against God, his participated being comes to deny, to contest God as the source that communicates Being.

CESANA: The second question came directly from Madrid: "What did you mean when you said that we must obey the authorities (I think you meant the civil authorities)? And in what sense does this not contradict what you had said before about the state as God-idol?"

FR PINO: There is no contradiction in the two points made, because what we wanted to strike at is the idolatrous claim of every authority that wants to base authority on itself, that is, to be the exclusive source of decision concerning the I. What we want to strike at is the state's claim to be the exclusive source of what the I is and of what the I can do.

Every authority – not only that of the state – even that of the Church, of husband and wife, of parents for their children, of the school, even that among friends – any authority, any power that claims to be founded exclusively on itself contains falsehood, to a greater or lesser extent, a deception, therefore it is inevitably a violence, precisely because it tends to be an absolute claim.

On the contrary, true authority is the point that cares for the other's destiny; the authority is good since – this was the conclusive passage yesterday – it cares for the common good and the possibility of destiny, therefore in as much as it accepts that the destiny of the I, and that the I itself have its origin elsewhere, be constituted by Another, be original by relationship with the Mystery.

It is only this, it is only the acknowledgment of this that can conquer the inevitable falsehood underlying every power to a greater or lesser extent.

CESANA: The third question: "What is meant by 'sin is to follow a stranger'?"

FR PINO: Sin is following a stranger, that is, following an attraction that does not lead towards destiny, an answer which is off the path. Sin is really following an answer that does not correspond to the desire for happiness, the desire for fulfilment that my heart is. It seems something normal, it seems something that can answer that desire, but no sooner do I follow it than I discover that the idol has a mouth and does not speak: it does not keep its promises. The extraneousness is precisely in respect to destiny, to the goal, to happiness: something that is outside, external to our happiness, that cannot accomplish it.

CESANA: And lastly, Pino, a practical question: "Does the imitation of Christ coincide with imitating the charism?"

FR PINO: The imitation of Christ is imitation of Christ, of his person. But for me, in the end, this would remain ultimately the content of a devotion or of a feeling, were it not to pass through the here and now of a face, a temperament, a history. For me the encounter with Christ has been with a face, a person. Christ, the man Jesus, in his contemporariness, in his here and now is, for us, the charisma, the historical locus through which Christ says: "Come and see."

CESANA: Now there are two fundamental questions for Fr Giussani, which relate to what was a very frequent request in the faxes we received: the relationship between the title "You, or about Friendship" and the lessons.

Many have asked to understand more. We have picked two questions that we think particularly meaningful from this point of view.

The first is: "We were particularly struck by the judgment given on the fact that the redeeming point of the I is first of all ontological rather than ethical, as the power attempts to make us believe. Is it possible to go deeper into this?"

The other question is: "It seems that what pertains to us is prayer defined as asking for being. I pray for many things I have at heart but what do you mean by 'asking for being'?"

GIUSSANI: The first question is about the relationship between onto-logical and ethical. Ontological is that for which a thing is real, as it is in reality, the way in which a thing is real.

If I need to use a spoon, excuse the comparison, but, if I have to use a spoon, I cannot pick it up by kicking it with my foot: I must pick it up with my hand, get a good grip on it. I cannot, for instance, get hold of the wrong end and then eat from the handle. Ethics derives from the consideration and the awareness of reality, from something in its reality, for it makes us behave as the thing requires. Otherwise, we can treat something wrongly, we can get hold of the wrong end of the stick, and miss the heart of the matter.

What was the second question?

CESANA: That we pray for many things, but what does it mean asking for being, praying to be? "I pray for many things I have at heart, but what do you mean by 'asking for being'?"

GIUSSANI: What you have at heart, my friend, is an answer that you will not receive completely till the end. What you have at heart is a mode with which you acknowledge in a partial and ephemeral, transitory, non-definitive, incomplete reality, that which is your only desire, or the sum-total of your desire, which is happiness.

This is why your asking for being stresses the fact that what you want, what you desire, what you ask for, is nothing but the request for the satisfaction that you expect to be total in a particular aspect of your person, of your life. If you expect the whole from a particu-lar, from holding the particular in your hand, you are mistaken.

CHRIST THE LIFE OF LIFE

1. "He Did and Taught"

We started with these two questions: what is God to man, and how can we know Him in this way, in as much as we say we know Him?

The first answer is ontological, that is, it starts from reality as it is, from the reality of God as He is, from what God is, in order to sug-gest, to find a suggestion regarding how we should behave towards this God. How can we know God in such a way that His reality may take on an ethical meaning for us, may show us how we can behave, what our behaviour should be in front of Him?

The starting point is ontological, it starts from reality as it is. For man, God is everything! And being, that which is, reality, is God; it is contained in the phrase "God is all," the whole of being. Outside God there is nothingness, not something else.

So, man truly acknowledges what God is only if in all that he does he entreats God for being – and every action is entreaty to God for being, that is for happiness, for being (everyone has a goal in which one will finally and totally be oneself). Every action is entreaty to God for being, that is, it is prayer, because every action of the I, as a phenomenon in which existence becomes true, by which the existence of the I comes true, is an attempt to affirm our own fulfilment.

"You [Christians]," Péguy said, "touch God everywhere."[70] Whatever we touch, whatever we enter into relationship with, we are looking for our fulfilment. Therefore, every awareness of an action, every time an action is aware, it is an entreaty to be, an entreaty to Being for being, an entreaty the participated being addresses to Being in order to be, in order to exist always, for all that he has received, for all that he is.

The second answer draws from the ontological discovery – God is all, and man is participated being, a self-communication of the Mystery which is Being – a matter of conscience, and of ethical conscience, that is, of behaviour. For, if God is a given reality, if God is all (there are no other words to be used), if God for man is everything, and He appears to reason as the source of being, but man does not understand, and does not remember, it is as if God were not there. For most of us every day that passes is filled up with this sin. The word "sin" is precise, but it carries not the bonhomie but the dejection of when we say, "Look, so and so has done this, what a pity! He has lost his common sense!" And similarly, for God, "He was not acknowledged, what a pity!"

How can we know Him in this way? How can we know with certainty and clarity that He is everything, so that man cannot act without asking for what he has already had from Him: being, participation in being, created being, that is, participated being?

How can we know Him? Well, we have to become aware of Him. Awareness concerns first of all the cognitive power rational man has. Reason is awareness of reality according to the totality of its factors. Therefore, becoming aware of something is to discover the object in question according to its totality, the object we are talking about, the object which interests me, the object on the agenda: God, how man conceives God, how God appears, how God must appear to man.

Thus reason, once it realizes that God is the source of everything, that the Mystery lies at the origin of everything, is also keen to discover how to behave towards God, how we should treat God, and therefore to discover the paths that lead on to the moral law.

But here we had to indicate a qualitative jump that is truly enigmatic.

The Mystery, source and destiny of the whole of created reality, wanted there to be a man born of woman, who lived through the human career as any man, the man Jesus of Nazareth, and, as He wanted to communicate Himself to men through this man, the Mystery made this man his own, from the first moment of his conception, mysteriously taking up the I of this man in the I of the Word, the second person of the Holy Trinity, and therefore directly sharing in God's nature: supreme mystery in the history of man and of the cosmos. This is why Jesus of Nazareth is "Jesus called the Christ."

Watching, listening to and following this man is the whole source of Christian morality. The Mystery wanted the man Jesus so that He might be first of all an instrument of teaching to all men, of the supreme teaching of life which is the teaching about God, the only Master ("Don't call yourselves masters, only one is your master. You are all disciples, brothers").[71] Therefore, in what He made, He was an example of what He said in a masterly way, of what he communicated as teaching: He did and taught. The Lord Jesus did and taught.

Speaking of God, we can only teach something which has preoccupied us, something that has occupied our soul, the whole of our soul before.

The most sublime thing about a moral attitude like that which Christ teaches us is that every action – as relationship with God, with Jesus, with the humanity of the individual and of society – is friendship. Every human relationship is either friendship or otherwise it lacks something, it is defective or false.

This is why the man Jesus said, "Father, if you are willing, take this cup away from me; still, not my will but yours be done."[72] Thus, He was both teacher and master, a teacher for all men, passing through His death, accepting death for men: "He who loved me and gave Himself up for me,"[73] St Paul said.

Every relationship is friendship in that it is a gift, it represents a gift or it has the possibility of being one, which comes from God, or from Christ, or from the Church, or from man's history: it is a gift, friendship, which we welcome. All that God, Christ, the Church, or the history of mankind as something communicable to all men gives us a gift we welcome and accept. Accepting and welcoming this gift makes reciprocal the love that He, who gave it to us, possesses, displays, and shows. Accepting it is the love that we show to Him who gave us the gift.

In this sense friendship is a reciprocity of gift, of love, because for a created being, like man, the supreme form of love for God is to accept that you are made by God, to accept to be, to accept being which is not one's own but is given.

2. An Event in the Present

The presence of Jesus Christ, which is in every day and every hour of the life of the baptized, of one who has been chosen by Him to whom the Father has given all men is an event.

The presence of Jesus Christ is for all mankind because the baptized person is one chosen as the passage, the point of communication of what God offers man, of the gift He makes of Himself to man, to the whole of mankind. Let us think, for instance of this in particular: if I am baptized, I was baptized so that the power of the Mystery which has transformed me in baptism, wanted to pass through me in order to reach others along many paths and occasions. This is the ontology of the new relationship with everything: the relationship between the baptized and the others comes from the aim that the Mystery, in baptism, gave us. The Mystery has begun to make us know, with the energy that He gave us in baptism, the aim He had in choosing us. This is the source of the ethics, the behaviour to be followed, that I must follow when I become aware of my baptism, which cannot be forgotten in any action; on no day, in no hour has man the right to forget this choice. The aim of this choice penetrates the whole organics of the human phenomenon, of the human gesture, of man's commitment: it penetrates everything in order to reach an aim that surpasses it on every side. In this sense we have always said that the instant has an eternal value, it is an enacted relationship with infinity, like the greatest action, the greatest epic, the greatest story.

So, the presence of Jesus Christ is an *event* – according to the perception given us (quite persuasively!) by our charism. It is an event that we encounter in the present, in the now, in circumstances, which spread the evidence of a vocational companionship as emergence of the mystery of the Church, the mysterious Body of Christ.

A supernatural reality is a human reality in which the mystery of Christ is present, a natural reality in which the mystery of Christ is present (natural in the sense that it shows itself and becomes specific in a human face). It is the Church that emerges close to me; it emerged close to me in precise circumstances, with my father and my mother, and then when I joined the seminary, and then when I began to meet people who became attentive and friendly to me because I was saying certain things, and, in the end, I was somehow channeled into a companionship that made and makes the mystery of the Church immediate for me. It is therefore an emergence of the Body of Christ. It is the company we call vocational, that is, the company that involves because it generates and is generated by the experience in which the charism has touched me.

St Augustine said: "*In manibus nostris sunt codices, in oculis nostris facta*"[74] (in our hands books, in our eyes facts). "*In manibus nostris sunt codices*": the Gospels to be read, the Bible to be read ... but we would not know how to read them without the other clause, "*in oculis nostris facta*": the presence of Jesus is nourished, comforted, proved by the reading of the Gospels and the Bible, but it is assured, it becomes evident among us through a fact, through facts that are presences. In the whole life of everybody there is a fact that has meaning, a presence which has been an influence throughout life, a presence tending to influence the whole of life: it has enlightened the way of conceiving, of feeling, of acting. This is called an event. That into which we are introduced stays truly alive, comes true every day, and so every day we become aware, we must become aware of the event as it happened to us, of the encounter we have had.

I conclude this confidential stressing of the points of my concern, by saying: Christ, this is the name that indicates and defines a reality I have encountered in my life. I have encountered: I heard of it when I was a child, as a boy, and so on. It is possible to grow up knowing the word Christ well, but for many people He is not encountered, He is not really experienced as being present. In my case Christ bumped into my life, my life bumped into Christ, precisely so that I should learn to understand that He is the central point of everything, of the whole of my life. *Christ is the life of my life*: in Him is summed up all that I would desire, all that I look for, all that I sacrifice, all that develops in me out of love for the persons with whom He has put me, that is, out of love for you.

As Möhler said in a sentence I have quoted many times, "I think I would not wish to live any longer if I could not hear him speak."[75] This is a sentence I wrote under Carracci's image of Christ when I was in high school. Perhaps it is one of the sentences I have remembered most in my life.

Christ, life of my life, certainty of a good destiny, and companionship in everyday life, a familiar companionship that transforms things into good. This is His efficacy in my life.

Then morality not only starts from here, but here the thread of morality is attached, fixed and saved.

St Peter did not take as the motive of his love for Christ the fact of having been forgiven his many defects, his many mistakes, his many betrayals. He did not list his own mistakes, but, when he found himself face to face with Christ after the resurrection, and when Christ asked him, "Simon, do you love me?" he answered, "Yes." It is the relationship with His word, which is the most human and the most divine, which makes us embrace everything in our daily existence. The memory of Him has to be daily, the surge with which He becomes familiar has to be daily, the company with Him has to become glad, and the memory of Him has to leave us glad, in whatever circumstance, in whatever condition, for there He is made flesh: in you, O Lord, the love the Mystery has for me is made flesh. A certainty of reaching my happy destiny and hope throughout the unfolding of my life.

"Yes, Lord, you know I love you." I might have made mistakes and betrayed a thousand times in thirty days, but this still stands, this must stand! I think that this is not a presumption, but a surprising, inconceivable yet ineffable grace, as Michelangelo Buonarroti said, "But, Lord, what am I to do if to my eye / no more Your ineffable courtesy appears?"[76]

Christ, and our "Yes" to Him: paradoxically I say, this is humanly the easiest aspect. I say this a bit presumptuously, and a bit enthusiastically: it is the easiest aspect, or, anyway, the most acceptable, of all the moral duty we have in the world. For Christ is the word that explains everything: Christ is a man who lived as everybody else two thousand years ago, but who, risen from the dead, invested by the power of the Mystery – in which by then He participated in His own nature – takes hold of us day after day, hour after hour, action after action.

The totality of the presence of the Mystery and its claim on our lives ("God is all in all") and of Christ, of Jesus of Nazareth, of the young man of Nazareth Jesus, who is the Mystery made Christ, His Christ, the totality of the one, of the great figure, of the enormous figure, of the enormous hint which God, which the word God is in our heart and on our lips, the totality of this familiar, daily, and efficacious presence of this company as strange as it is evidently insuperable. This totality explains our "You." To God we must say, "You," and "You, O Christ," we must say to the man Jesus of Nazareth.

Both the Mystery and His physical presence in our life, all of this is the source of the relationship we have with the truth and with the whole of reality, and it also becomes the source of what we have called friendship. There is no relationship before You, O Christ, whenever I encounter You thinking of You in the memory of You, I can have no human relationship, of any kind, with anyone, without the theme, the ideal of friendship being pursued. You looked at all those to whom you spoke, or who answered You, or with whom there was no dialogue at all, even Pilate, even the Jewish high priests; the relationship You had with them was full, as it is proved by your passion, it was full of passion for their destiny, for the destiny of their persons, and your involvement with them presented you as being full of love for them. If they had welcomed, if they had come to agree with you, the word friendship would have been the only one they could have used for the relationship with You. The word friendship is the only one we can use for our relationship with Him.

St Maximus the Confessor, a great father of the Church, gives us this admirable summary, that we quoted above:

> Christ is [...] all in all of us [whether we are good or bad, whether we are distracted, whether we are offside or inside], He who embraces everything in Himself according to the unique, infinite, and most wise power of his bounty, as a centre into which all lines converge [all the lines of creation: this is the ontological birth, the gaze of ontology from which all our attitude in life must be born] – so that the creatures of the one God may not remain strangers and enemies to each other, but have a common locus where they can manifest their friendship and their peace.[77]

This is the synthesis of the spirit with which we have spoken and thought during these days.

The Miracle of a Change

(1998)

"A New Beginning," read the cover of the magazine *Tracce* in its first issue of the year, referring to the presentation of the book *The Religious Sense* to the United Nations in New York. Like "St Peter's mission in Rome,"[1] Fr Giussani commented, underlining the two-fold character of the Christian mission: the freedom to confront even the most difficult circumstances ("at the heart of the empire"); and the renewal of the I as a subject, which makes the event of Christ present.

That year's Fraternity Exercises were dedicated to that conversion which changes a human being at its very root. The deepening of one's self-awareness, then, was closely linked to one's perception of the judgment faith brings to the world. An interpretation of modernity, in its contrasting aspects – "the prevalence of ethics over ontology";[2] nihilism and skepticism; violence, and, on the other hand, the continual emergence of possibilities for good and for truth that could inspire true ecumenism – frequently appeared in his meditations just as it appeared in his public articles in the press. It had been a few years already that major daily newspapers had been inviting Fr Giussani somewhat regularly to send articles and letters, and a wide range of readers had begun to get to know him more closely, appreciating his value and overcoming unfounded prejudices.

His passion for encounter and dialogue with others gave rise to another series of texts entitled, "QuasiTischreden" resurrecting a classic European tradition of publishing spontaneous and free conversations among friends on issues related to life, faith, and engagement in society.

A love for music – "he grew up in a poor home [...] as far as bread was concerned but rich with music,"[3] recounted Cardinal Ratzinger about Giussani's childhood – inspired Fr Giussani to launch a successful CD music series ("Spirto Gentil"), which introduced many people to some of the most beautiful and intense examples of singing, melody, and works of music.

In April, Fr Giussani participated in the CLU Equipe for the last time, after having closely followed what he considered to be the most vibrant place in the movement's experience for over twenty years. He spoke of "Leopardi's journey"[4] and extended an invitation that had the sound of handing over the torch: "Bring this dynamic [...] of the main reason for our friendship to fulfilment yourselves: [...] this fulfilment of the heart, of the needs of the heart, without which nihilism would be the only possible conclusion."[5]

This blossoming of humanity and initiative was the surprising rebound in the face of Giussani's ever-more precarious physical health, which made speaking, among other things, more difficult. His concrete circumstances were such that they could have halted him, representing an obstacle or even an objection, but they were instead considered as, "an essential and not secondary factor of our vocation."[6] Illness brought Fr Giussani even closer to John Paul II, whom he on several occasions, both in public and in private, referred to as a "father and teacher," and whom he supported in preparation for the great Jubilee Year of 2000, which became the object of controversy and critique from the press.

This year, too, the meditations for the Exercises were recorded a number of days in advance. Giussani's reflections on the nature of faith and the intellectual context of the modern age reached a surprising depth and clarity: the "three reductions" of Christianity and the "five withouts" of modern rationalism would become essential articles of Christian self-awareness.

Fr Giussani was present at the Exercises and participated in the assembly, answering questions and explaining passages that participants had not understood well. It was the beginning of a long process of understanding that would continue for many years.

Around ten European countries followed the meditations and the assembly live by satellite connection; and another twenty-four non-European countries, in different time zones, watched and listened to the recordings hours later.

For a number of years, and for years to follow, Saturday's Eucharistic celebration was presided over by the President of the Pontifical Council for the Laity, who also gave the homily: first Cardinal Eduardo F. Pironio, then Cardinal James F. Stafford, and finally Archbishop Stanisław M. Ryłko. It was a significant sign of the care the Church and, in a particular way, the Pope had for movements, and of the ecclesial authorities' appreciation of what sprung up from the grassroots as an essential gift for the entire Church.

At the end of the month of May, the World Congress of Ecclesial Movements and New Communities took place in Rome. It concluded with a meeting in St Peter's Square with the Pope. In his opening address, Cardinal Ratzinger spoke of his encounter with movements as a "wonderful event" during years of "winter" in the Church.[7] John Paul II underlined the co-essentiality of both the institutional and charismatic aspects in the Church. In his witness in St Peter's Square, Fr Giussani emphasized that, "the real protagonist of history is the beggar: Christ who begs for man's heart, and man's heart that begs for Christ."[8] He later remembered 30 May of that year as "the greatest day in the history of the Movement."[9]

GOD AND EXISTENCE

1. A Problem of Knowledge

"God is all in all."[10] How does this become valid, or come to have an impact on life? For an assertion that has no impact on life is abstract, it remains abstract, or appears rather absurd. The first thing I would like to say is that "God is all in all" is the striking consequence that reason leads to, at least when reason is understood according to the realistically natural experience we have of it, as a healthy and adequate philosophy of man affirms it. Let's not forget that reason, for us, is the need for a total meaning, it is openness to reality according to the totality of its factors. That "God is all in all" is a deep expression of reason for us, an opportunity to fully affirm its value; it is not an absurd formulation, nor is it an abstract one. It can simply be judged, understood, or not understood, as a real factor of life.

So, if "God is all in all" we have to see how this has an impact on our life. How can we become aware of it? What do we mean by becoming aware of it? It means in the first place knowing God in such a way that He has an impact on life. For Being reveals itself in as much as it is at work in our present: it is, if it is at work before our eyes. Therefore, knowing him implies a change, and the first connotation of this is the change in the image that human intelligence describes to us as it works. The first important element for an ethically dignified construction, the first important factor for a will for one's own transformation, in order that our presence be more useful in the world and for the world, is therefore in the order of knowledge. Before doing, before getting to work, it is a problem of knowledge. The activity of the intelligence expresses the *mens* of the subject in as much as it creates a new, precise point for approaching everything: in this sense, *facta sunt omnia nova* (all things are made new).[11]

We need to become aware of the ethical consequences for which "God is all in all," and even before of the aesthetic force by which God is truly "all in all." The very possibility of an ethics is born from this aesthetic force; only if Being is attractive can it engage man's attention up to the point of sacrifice. Every day we are asked nothing more than to preserve faithfully and loyally our desire and will to be humble and obedient before the greatness of the Being who makes us. In order to become aware then, of such ethical consequences, we must take note of a way of thinking that, apparently exalting a religious re-birth, in point of fact wants to censure the fact that "God is all in all," feeling it abstractly, or forgetting it, or going as far as denying it. So, we need to take note of the reality in which we are living, of the cultural moment of our journey – cultural in the strong sense of the word.

It is impossible to live in a general cultural context without coming under its influence. We, too, share in the way of thinking in which God is conceived abstractly, or forgotten, or even denied. Thus, in practice, existentially, we come to deny that "God is all in all." In our restless and confused spirit, the falsehood of the modern-day way of thinking is present, in which we ourselves participate, because we are children of this historical reality that is human life and we have to pass through all the hardships, the temptations, the bitter consequences, and keep that hope that is the life of life. Let's measure the falsehood that is in us, how much falsehood has entered into us from the world in which we live.

2. *Experience and Reason*

The denial of the fact that "God is all in all," resulted from an irreligiosity foreign to the formation of the European peoples.

There is an irreligiosity in our world that began – without anyone realizing it – in a separation that was operated between God as the origin and meaning of life (therefore pertinent to the things that happen, the events we undergo) and God as a fact of thought, of human thinking, conceived according to the needs of human thought. This stems from a separation of the meaning of life from experience. Denial of God to the point of denying the reasonably extreme and evident consequence that "God is all in all," implies a separation of the meaning of life from experience, because the meaning of life is God. Experience is the relationship between man's freedom and the reality in which he finds himself immersed. If God is conceived of as separated from experience, if God has no impact on life, then we have a separation of the meaning of life from experience. In other words, the meaning of life has no longer any relationship or has a relationship that is difficult to define with the moment of existence in which one is actually walking. You can't break the relationship between the step man is taking in this moment and the meaning of everything, the reason why he is moving. And why is he walking? And where to? He is walking towards the meaning of life and towards his destiny.

The separation of the meaning of life from experience also implies a separation between morality and man's action: thus, morality does not have the same root as action. In what way? In the sense that morality is certainly linked with man's action, with his experience, but in such a way that it does not have the same root as the action, and doesn't correspond to the physiognomy, the face that our experience gives us.

In this way, amongst other things, we can understand how moralism was born. Paradoxically moralism is morality that has nothing to do with action in the sense that action and morality are not born in the same moment. Moralism is morality seen as a collection of principles that impinge on man's action, judging it theoretically, abstractly, without giving reasons for why it is right or wrong, and why man should or should not do it. In defining the action that man is doing, morality judges it. It judges what man is doing without man's being aware of it, or without his having conceived his acting in the world, the ways he walks though time and space as practicable means. Thus, morality does not have the same root as action. So morality stresses common values, values that are felt by society; its adequate principles are either the common mentality or imposition by the state.

The heart of the matter becomes clear in the dispute over how to read and analyze the relationship between reason and experience. To understand it you just need to look at the formulation "God is all in all" that shatters the most common formulation of God's existence ("God exists"). For the affirmation of a supreme Being is always calmly accepted, the existence of God fixed in Himself with no relationship with man's action, except at the end as a judge which approves or destroys what man has done. In the way of conceiving the relationship between reason and experience, the order of the great plan of God, which is the cosmos, is threatened in its very roots. Morality reduced to moralism marks the relationship between the order of the plan of God and the event of human action as an ideal preconception. It is rather through experience that man shows his adherence, by connecting his action to the global plan, to the totality, or his denying it, by not responding to such a clearly ultimate and decisive reference.

Jean Guitton, by identifying us to be in this restless unease of ours, encouraged us, to make us feel the correctness of our attitude as regards the relationship between reason and life when he said, "to be reasonable is to subject reason to experience."[12] Experience is the emergence of reality to man's consciousness, it is reality becoming transparent to man's gaze. So, reality is something that you come across, it is a datum, and reason is that level of creation in which creation becomes aware of itself. It is not a philosophy, but an existential necessity. Why is it "reasonable to subject reason to experience?" Because it is experience that tells us the reality that we are, in which we are present, and it is a reality that we are given, that we come across. We come across it, we don't create it ourselves, we don't invent it ourselves. However, reason is that level of creation in which creation becomes aware of itself, by becoming conscious, therefore, of the datum, of that *something* man comes across. This self-awareness generates the definition of reason.

In order to defend God in his truth and in order to defend the need for man to conceive his life as His and to tend in everything to please this supreme creator and manager of all that exists, we need to recover the word reason from our heart. It is the word that is most confused in modern day discourse. If the word reason is used wrongly then all man's knowledge as a building on reality, of reality, is put in jeopardy. If the word reason is used wrongly, that is to say, if reason is understood as a measure of reality – and this always implies reason as a preconception, as something that would have a strange effect on experience, in order to reduce it and not recognize what is present in our lives – there are three possible serious reductions that affect all our behaviour in life. It is this threefold reduction that lets us see and understand the profound difference there is between a Christian culture and a profane, non-Christian culture.

To speak of a culture means speaking of the whole human approach of our presence in the world, because culture is not an outcome sought by those who are enthusiastic or competent: culture is that from which man draws his whole way of behaving, that from which he draws inspiration for his way of behaving as the origin of everything, in formulating and in explaining it, following the evolution of things and of life, and in the affirmation of the ultimate aim of what he does, that is to say, his destiny.

If reason is used wrongly, if it is used as the measure of things, this brings about three possible reductions that affect all our behaviour. So, if we have to speak of morality, it is of the greatest importance that we understand and take stock of the type of culture we are part of, whether it is a worldly culture or a Christian culture.

3. Three Serious Reductions

a) First reduction – I am describing the genesis of our behaviour in its dramatic and contradictory aspect: *ideology in place of an event.*

Either the relationship with reality that man lives from morning to evening is a continuous initiative, a continuous attempt as regards what happens and what he experiences, or he is moved, and allows himself to be moved by something that is not born, that does not spring from his own way of reacting to the things he meets, the things he comes across, but from preconceptions.

For the Christian the starting point is an event. The starting point for everything else in human thought is a particular impression of things, a particular evaluation of things, a particular attitude one takes up before tackling things, above all before judging them: even human needs, that man intercepts and tries to share concretely, can be thought of and conceived of in a preconceived way, in a way that produces a preconception. To take the example of a disastrous railway or mining accident. The way of tackling these facts that question man is not born, or tends not to be born, of a human reverberation, of what man feels as man before these events. Without man realizing it, it is as if something intruded into his judgment, an argument he has heard, something he has experienced; he starts from a preconception. So it is that the liberal- or republican-biased newspaper will report it in one way, while the newspaper favouring the government will take a different view. And the preconception, that is, the starting point for one's argument, in order to go down in history, to endure in time, to score points in the fields of public opinion and the judgment of society, needs to be developed. Its development is through the logic of a discourse that becomes ideology. The logic of a discourse that starts off from a preconception and wants to impose it is called ideology.

If, on the contrary, the origin, the foundation, the founding principle of the whole of human experience, is an event – the only true alternative to preconception is something that happens, something that man comes across – if the criterion that suggests man's behaviour is an event, then this event is recomposed in history, in time, day after day, hour after hour. This event is understood because something is happening now. Memory is the opposite of ideology.

Our life of faith, our life as Christians in front of the world, is an important alternative of which we are not aware if we don't pay attention to the one whom God has placed as guide for His Church. A famous page of Alexis Carrel reminds us of this: "Few observations and much discussion are conducive to error [and to dissolution]: much observation and little discussion to truth [that is they keep real contact with what is]."[13] Our Christian life, our faith, and our concrete morality, the set-up of our lives is determined either by current ideologies or by the factuality, the supremacy of our existence, of things as they happen, of things as we come across them, of things with which you react in a given way, of facts: facts as events. The birth of a child, for example, is an event. There are events that are great and events that are of the tiniest significance.

If then, the origin, the foundation, the founding principle of the whole of human experience is an event, then this event is understood, makes itself understood, because in some way it is happening now. We cannot speak of a past that is decisive for a person who is living today if that past doesn't in some way become present. If it is purely a remembrance – but it can't just be a remembrance – let it pass away, but, if it is not purely a remembrance, it is something of the past and affects the present. Thus, Christianity is an event and is therefore present, it is present now, and its characteristic is that it is present as a memory, and Christian memory is not the same as a remembrance, or better, it is not a remembrance, but the re-happening of the Presence itself.

Only the recognition of this event prevents us from being slaves to any ideology. All ideologies have a system of argument and in the logic that supports them they tend to grab power or they have power (everyone can be blocked by ideology), since power is one ideology that prevails over the others in that particular moment.

Christianity, on the contrary, is born as an event that becomes flesh in the present as memory.

b) This leads us to a second reduction that is culturally significant and ethically grave. Ethically grave because ethics, in as much as it derives from aesthetics, in as much as it is launched along the path of its journey by an aesthetic factor, implies a grandiose definition of the concept of Being, in other words, of the concept of God.

The reduction that takes place for man, in so far as he gives in to the dominant ideologies that emerge from the common mentality, is a division, a separation, the struggle between sign and appearance, and as a consequence *the reduction of sign to appearance*. The more we realize what a sign is, the more we understand how vile and disastrous it is to reduce a sign to appearance.

The sign is the experience of a factor, a presence in reality that refers to something else. A sign is an experienceable reality whose meaning is another reality, a reality that can be experienced; it acquires its meaning by leading to another reality.[14]

It would not be reasonable, nor human, then, to exhaust the experience of the sign by interpreting it only in its perceptively immediate aspect or appearance. The perceptively immediate aspect of a thing, of anything, its appearance, does not tell the whole experience of the things that we are looking at, because it does not tell us the sign-value.

Man's great temptation is to exhaust the experience of the sign, of something that is a sign, by interpreting it solely in its perceptively immediate aspect. It is not reasonable, but all men tend, thanks to the burden of original sin that weighs upon all of us, to fall prey to appearances, to what appears, because it seems the easiest form of reason. A certain attitude of spirit makes you behave more or less like this towards the reality of the world and of existence (the circumstances, the relationship with things, to start a family, bring up your children): it feels the rub, blocking your human capacity to search for meaning that our relationship with reality inevitably solicits in our intelligence. Thus, our human capacity is blocked, that capacity of the intelligence that is at work to go in search of meaning that our relationship with what we come across, with reality inevitably arouses. Human intelligence cannot come across something without perceiving that in some way it is a sign of another reality, that it is suggestive of another reality.

These concepts of ours, which we are accustomed to, can be perceived by reading an affirmation of that famous Jewish thinker, Hannah Arendt, in her *The Origins of Totalitarianism*: "Ideology [...] is not the naïve acceptance of what is visible, but the knowledgeable dismissal of it."[15] Ideology is the destruction of what is visible, the elimination of what is visible as the meaning of what happens, the emptying of what we see, of what we touch, of what we perceive. You no longer have a relationship with anything. When Sartre speaks of his hands – "My hands, what are my hands?" He defines them as: "The immense distance that separates me from the world of objects, and separates me from them forever,"[16] bringing about a destitution of what is visible, of the contingent aspect. Destitution of what is contingent is, for example, affirming that what happens, happens just because it happens, avoiding the shock, the need to look at the present in its relationship with the whole.

The concept of sign, on the other hand, operationally brings the meaning of things into life.

Mystery (in other words, God) and sign (in other words, contingent reality in as much as it always recalls something else: even the tiniest stone, in order to be itself, has to be conceived of as made by God, has to be a reminder of the source of Being), Mystery and sign, in a certain sense coincide: in the sense that the Mystery is the depth of the sign, the sign points to the presence of the deep Mystery, of God the Creator and the Redeemer, of God the Father. The sign indicates the presence of the Mystery, of the deep Mystery – Mystery is the depth of the sign – it points out to our eyes the presence of something Other, of the deep Mystery for all things, it points it out to our eyes, to our ears, to our hands. The Mystery becomes an experience through the sign.

Therefore, sensitivity in perceiving all things as a sign of the Mystery is the tranquil truth of the human being, whereas tyranny, which becomes the possession of those who hold power, motivated by an ideology, denies this consideration that man has for something. Even things that happen, even events then become so fleeting in their contingency that they don't dictate any change in life; they don't suggest anything more expressive in life.

Ideology tends to affirm what is apparent as concrete, but what is apparent is what is seen, what is heard, what is touched. Whereas the way of looking that is properly human is reason: reason that invests the contact that the I has with what it comes across. It leaves it intact but clarifies it and judges it, in other words, it makes it refer to something else, because you can judge it only if there is the hypothesis of a depth.

So, Mystery and sign in a certain sense coincide and the Mystery becomes experience through the sign. This explains to the Christian the value of the sacraments, when he discovers that the whole of reality is built of this method of God, the Creator. Reality comes from the Creator, having within it a reference to the Creator, which it demonstrates. In the intimacy of our relationship with things, it brings out the perception of Another, of something Other.

The sacrament is different from all the other signs. In the sacraments invented, or created by Christ, with the purpose of generating a new people in the world – that flows like a river into the waters of the sea of mankind, that flows like the initial revelation within history of the infinite Mystery that man will go to meet at the end of his days: it is the beginning, in history, of eternity – in the sacraments, created by Christ, created by the God-man, by God who became man, Jesus of Nazareth (He was the one who made them, He was the one who suggested them), in the sacraments the sign reaches the point of complete identity with the Mystery; as in the Eucharist. But this totalizing reference is in all the sacraments: the sign coincides with the Mystery in the real sense. The sacraments make this present: from baptism, which is a total transformation of our being, to the Eucharist, which is an expressive fullness of this coincidence, to penance, to the identification with a task in holy orders and matrimony. Thus, in the sacrament man is washed clean of the scales that hold him prisoner and tend to make him live like an animal.

This is why in our life we take sides against the triumph of appearances over the perspective that the sign offers, we are in the fight for a new, a more perfect morality, a morality of which Christ says, "I didn't come into the world to destroy the law, but to support it, so that it be more complete."[17] It is man's salvation: we could say: "If I had not met you Christ, I would no longer be a man." The Rhetor Gaius Marius Victorinus said, "When I met Christ I realized I was a man."[18]

The sacramental method is the way in which the Mystery gives itself, gives itself to nothingness, creating its cosmos, persons and his cosmos. The method with which God communicates His existence, gives His Being, shares His Being, is the sacramental method, it is sacramentality: the Mystery's communicating itself implies a sacramental method. Everything is a sign of Him, and the last border of this method, following an analogy amongst things, between the meanings of things, is given by the sacrament of his presence in the world, because every sacrament is the presence of Christ died and risen in the world. How much our spiritual life has to be disposed consciously around the sacrament! In fact, what is changed under the impulse, the light, and the tenderness of baptism and the other sacramental signs is called Church, mystical Body of Christ.

God conceived the relationship with creation as the relationship with a great army of signs – everything is a sign of Him, everything. Christ came to tell us this, because God wanted everything from us. So, reality, made as a sign of God, leads everything back to the vision of Christ. Treating creation well, using it well, means knowing Christ in order to know God. This is the beginning of a change in man.

c) The elimination of the value of sign implies – I don't know whether more as a cause or an effect – *the reduction of the heart to feelings.*

We take our feelings instead of our heart as the ultimate motor, as the ultimate reason for our actions, our feelings rather than our heart. What does this mean? This is precisely how our responsibility becomes irresponsible: we give in and use our feelings in place of our heart, thus reducing the concept of the heart to feelings. The heart on the other hand acts as the fundamental factor of the human personality. Feelings do not, because taken on their own feelings act as a reactivity, after all they are animalistic. Pavese said, "I do not yet understand what the tragedy of existence may be […] but this point is so clear. I must overcome this luxurious indulgence and stop regarding states of soul as an end in themselves."[19] In order to keep its dignity, a mood has a higher aim; its aim consists in its being a condition given by God, the Creator, through which purification takes place, while the heart indicates the unity of feeling and reason. It implies a concept of reason that is not blocked, a reason according to the full extent of its own possibility: reason cannot act without what is called affectivity.

It is the heart, as reason and affectivity, which is the condition necessary for the healthy realization of reason. The condition necessary in order for reason to be reason is that affectivity take hold of it and thus move the whole man. Reason and feelings, reason and affectivity: this is man's heart.

4. The Corruption of Religiosity

Up to now I wanted to stress the fact that in some way the conception of life according to which we live, the conception of life within whose terms we live, what inspires us to act in a particular way, or to reach a certain edification of our existence and our life in common with others, finds in reason its weapon both for attack and defence. We cannot start off except from a love for reason, from a trust in reason, and this has made us perceive the value of reason as the first thing to clarify.

In the second place, I intended to stress the attitude of today's world, the world that Jesus speaks of as "all steeped in lies."[20] The lie is to say, "God exists, but 'God is all in all' is abstract." What does it mean? What it amounts to is a denial of God, because all those who deny "God is all in all" actually deny God. This situation that I described above, characterizes the cultural and social – cultural and therefore social – trend, the political trend of our time. A long process has managed, slowly and inexorably, to implant certain preconceptions, certain preconceived principles, certain indications of preconceived activity in everyone's mind.

At the end of a long process of forgetfulness that "God is all in all," in this last century, the religious sentiment proper to human nature asserts itself with a freedom that is absurd, decaying as it does in the progressive elimination of the religiosity proper of Christ and therefore of the religiosity that has had, in a wonderful way, its manifestation and exemplification, the exemplification of its truth, of its extreme implications in the history of the Hebrew people. Just as the Hebrew people was mistreated by its enemies, by those who would not accept God as the one God who made all things, so the modern-day situation is averse to the religiosity proper to Christ, the heir to the whole humanly incomprehensible phenomenon of the Hebrew people – the history of the Hebrew people was the prophetic realization of what Christ was to clarify in Himself. This religiosity is the one we are to live. So, the fight in us is between the religiosity proper to Christ and the Bible, the Christian, the Hebrew tradition, and the god of the anti-Christian.

The denial of "God is all in all" reveals the presence of an anti-christianity in the formation of man and therefore of society; this denial leads to the elimination of the religious sense proper to Christ and to the Church and therefore of humanity that it invades and that receives it.

This incomprehension was favoured in the Church herself, since her pastors and her baptized members are affected, let themselves be affected by another culture. This can be seen as regards the question of missionary promotion, both on a personal level and at the level of society. Missionary promotion, which is, after all, the ultimate aim of each one's existence and of the trends of all the changes in society, reached an *impasse*, which peaked in the period of pre-conciliar and post-conciliar criticism. This criticism went so far as to claim that we should be afraid that missionary activity be against human freedom, whereas it is in fact the ultimate outcome, the extreme fruit of faithfulness to Christ.

In his "Letter to the Christians of the West," which will never be read and re-read often enough, Josef Zvěřina – the great Czech theologian, condemned for so many years by the Prague regime, and one of the most valid and sadly rare theologians the Church could count among its defenders – wrote in 1970:

> Brothers, You have the presumption of being useful to the
> Kingdom of God assuming as far as possible the *saeculum*,
> its life, its words, its slogans, its way of thinking. But reflect, I
> beg you, what it means to accept this world. Perhaps it means
> that you have gradually lost yourselves in it? Sadly, it seems
> you are doing just that. It is difficult these days to find you
> and recognize you in this strange world of yours. Probably we
> still recognize you because in this process you are taking your
> time, because you are being assimilated by the world, whether
> quickly or slowly, but late all the same. We thank you for many
> things, or rather for almost everything, but we must distinguish
> ourselves from you in one thing. We have much to admire in
> you, so we can and must send you this warning. "Do not con-
> form to this world [St Paul says], but transform yourselves by
> the renewal of your minds, so that you will be able to recognize
> the will of God, what is good, what is pleasing to him, what is
> perfect" (Rom. 12:2) ["God all in all," we say and suggest].

Do not conform! *Mé syschematizesthe*! How well this expression reveals the perennial root of the verb: schema. In a nutshell, all schemas, all exterior models are empty [if they do not stem from faith, from the experience of faith]. We have to want more, the apostle makes it our duty, "change your way of thinking, reshape your minds!" [...] He opposes *schèma* or *morphé* – permanent form – to *metamorphé* – change in the creature [*skhêma* or *morphé* mean a permanent form, affirm a permanent form; *meta-morphé* affirms something that is intended to change, that changes, that produces a continuous change in the creature]. One is not to change according to any model that in any case is always out of fashion, but it is a total newness with all its wealth [as Christ is]. It's not the vocabulary that changes but the meaning.

We cannot imitate the world precisely because we have to judge it, not with pride and superiority, but with love, just as the Father loved the world (Jn. 3:16) and for this reason pronounced judgment on it. [Christ, His judgment is Christ. And the Pope, in his encyclical *Dives in misericordia*, says that mercy in human history has a name: Jesus Christ. God's judgment is mercy].

We write as unwise men to you who are wise, as weak men to you who are strong, as wretched men to you who are even more wretched! And this is stupid of us because there are certainly among you some excellent men and women. But precisely for this reason we need to write foolishly, as the Apostle Paul taught us, when he took and repeated Christ's words, that the Father has hidden wisdom from those who know a lot about these things (Lk. 10:21)."[21]

This explains how the lack of understanding of the problem was facilitated in the Church – the problem of Christian education, of mission, of conversion, of the building of the Church. These problems require a change, they start off from a change that must happen in man; through a change that has come about in other men whom he meets, a Christian is helped to perceive and to pursue a change in himself. The miracle is this change in oneself.

5. Tradition and Charism

Faithfulness to Christ and to Tradition have to be sustained and strengthened by an ecclesial ambit that is truly aware of this necessary fidelity. This then is the conclusive point of my observations.

The ecclesial ambit, which is necessary so as to sustain and comfort us, has to be truly aware of what fidelity to Christ and to tradition means, of how truly to live Christian memory, and not the mere memory of the dead. Hence the moral impressiveness of the participation to an ecclesial movement, as a belonging to an ambit in which the gift of the Spirit that comes from baptism becomes concrete in forms that are demonstrative and persuasive. This gift of the Spirit is called *charism*. But it is no charism if it is not recognized by the authority of the Church, that is, by the Pope.

This invitation to live the gift we have received with full awareness has as its first moral consequence an attention with wholehearted readiness to the indications the movement gives: the belonging to the movement, lived with simplicity and generosity, is the source of light and comfort for the whole of our lives. As a matter of fact, belonging to the movement introduces, facilitates, or ensures a new mentality and commits you in a new morality. Since belonging to the movement is an essentially concrete experience of living the new mentality in Christ and the new morality, it introduces us into the novelty of a faith, that faith that tends to fail in men's hearts when the one immediately leading them betrays. This is what Julien Benda calls the *trahison des clercs*, the betrayal of the intellectuals. The intellectual is the one who teaches or educates, or the doctor who helps, who takes action.

There is no other way in which the Spirit can come to meet us more simply, more persuasively, more powerfully, than in a present reality, in a present context.

This is in no way contradictory to the obedience we owe to the bishop or to the parish priest. It is rather a factor that throws light on this obedience, it supports this obedience; an obedience moreover that is inherent in the very dynamics of the faithfulness to Christ and to the tradition that it demands. For a charism recognized by the Church is a gift of the Spirit of Christ that brings you to live the institution in a global way, as the locus in which Christ is a present event. John Paul II said: "An authentic movement therefore exists as a nourishing soul within the Institution. It is not a structure that is alternative to it. It is rather the wellspring of a presence which continually regenerates the Institution's existential and historical authenticity."²² A priest who is living this belonging to the movement in a lively and intelligent way, with his way of living and strengthening the parish with support from others, makes it become beautiful and simple.

On another occasion the Pope went to the heart of this judgment: "In the Church both the institutional aspect and the charismatic aspect [...] are coessential and work together for life, for renewal, and for sanctification, in different ways."²³ The charism, when followed with fidelity, introduces to fidelity of Christ through the fidelity to the institutions. So, charism and institution are co-essential in the definition of the Christian life of the Church, of ecclesial life. So, a movement is exemplary and demonstrative, it is persuasive in the dioceses and parishes themselves and useful for pastoral life.

The way of living the gift of the Spirit has to reach every single person in a capillary way. It is precisely in order to remind us of this that the Spirit calls everyone to one charism or another. All the charisms recognized by the Holy Church are co-essential to the Christian institution.

You truly live the charism the more you compare the whole of your life with the charism's own ideal, as it is affirmed by those who are recognized by the Church as the guarantors on her behalf of the truth of the Spirit's gift; following them is an ultimate obedience that tries to incarnate the imitation of Christ and fidelity to the Church down to the last capillaries. Faith thus reveals itself as a continuous source and as a continuous terminus of the Incarnation as the Mystery's ultimate method. Since mission exists and lives as witness, only a lived faith brings about mission, because only faith that is lived brings a change, the kind of change that anyone can come across and be shocked by it, and start following. This shows how faith opens one up to a new way of thinking and a new kind of morality, both as regards the world and as regards the Church herself as a human reality that can therefore be affected by the context.

What changes in us, through the intervention of the movement in our lives and out of the coherence that it demands, should begin consciously, reasonably, and should have knowledge as the first locus of the event, because all that man does depends on the way he conceives. So, it is a way of cognition that can limit or eliminate this conception that the world passes on to us according to which God is dealt with in the wrong way, He is not asserted as He wants to assert himself, because God asserts Himself in Christ. We cannot know the Mystery unless Christ tells us of Him. And the Church – this is an analogy not blasphemy – brings about Christ with greater clarity, more persuasively and with a life-giving support, through the movements. The Spirit of Christ who has created the Church and sent her into the world, comforts and builds her, fortifies her with charisms. The Spirit takes in certain people, in one charism or another, so that the whole Church be rejuvenated and reborn with awareness before everyone's eyes.

FAITH IN GOD IS FAITH IN CHRIST

1. A New Mentality

Faith opens us up to a different mentality from that into which we plunge every morning as we get up and leave home, but even at home, too. A new mentality (mentality is the point of view from which man starts off for all his activity), and, therefore, a new morality, because the activity through which man realizes himself may be more or less (or not at all) related with the totality of things. Now since reason is awareness of reality according to the totality of its factors, then, by analogy, morality is the relationship of the individual action with the totality of the relationships that the universe requires. Faith opens us up to a new mentality and a new morality, both as regards the world and in the Church herself as a human reality and therefore subject to the influence of worldly reality.

"Christ is all and in all"; let us take up this thematic formula and ask ourselves what impact it has on our life. "Christ is all and in all" means that the behaviour of Jesus of Nazareth – His relationship with the Father, the Mystery of the Father, that started off from a knowledge He had of the Father – has to affect everyone's life, has to be imitated by every man.

We, too, have to be before the Father just like Jesus. Our general theme, then, is "Christ is all and in all" so that "God may be all in all." The synthetic formula we need to develop is then: *faith in God is faith in Christ*. We shall see how the serious meaning of this assertion affects life. In order to understand what this means for human life and for human history, each of us has to get to know Christ, try to identify with Him, to imitate and follow Christ, Jesus Christ. The first effect on the life of a man who has this imitation of Christ

(Christ must be "all and in all") is a new mentality, a new awareness that cannot be reduced to any law of the state or social custom; a new awareness as the source and echo of a working relationship with reality, in all the details implicit in existence.

The worldly mentality puts all its deception to work on the global horizon of that to which man educates himself to as he grows. The new mentality finds it hard to take the place of this and has to fight for it. The new mentality, the new awareness of the Christian, of the imitator of Christ, is called to answer when faced with what the dominant mentality says. For the latter bases its whole deception on the claim that you can talk of God without involving Christ. This is the principle of the relationship with reality that defines the opposition between Christ and the world. "Christ entered the world in controversy with the world,"[24] Mgr Garofalo said. But we would say that He didn't enter the world "in controversy" with the world, but He entered the world revealing and communicating Himself, His Mystery. So, He came as a proposal, and it is the world that rises up against him.

The presumption of the dominant mentality is that one can talk of God without involving Christ. But as regards the Mystery, what we have been given, what has been communicated to us by the Mystery Itself, what we have been given in Revelation is the man Jesus Christ. This man is the synthesis and the centre of all the self-communication that the Mystery thought good to do towards His human creature. This is why the Word became flesh. Jesus once said, "Philip, whoever has seen me has seen the Father."[25] We cannot know God except through Christ.[26] There is no knowledge of the Mystery that is not a reductive human interpretation, except in that Man, Jesus of Nazareth, whom God assumed into his own nature in order to say Himself to man, to communicate Himself to man as Mystery. Man and Mystery: this was Jesus, this is Jesus, and this will be Jesus. "Christ, yesterday, today and forever."[27]

Faith, as a real attitude that man lives before God, is not something generic: it is *faith in Christ*, the Sign of all signs, the Man through whom the Mystery has revealed itself. After all, Jesus was a man like all the others, He was a man with nothing exceptional to the definition of man, a man like all the others. But Jesus said things of Himself that others didn't say; He said things and acted in a way that others didn't. The Sign of all signs. Once people got to know His reality, once they were struck by His claim, they looked at Him and treated Him as the sign of someone else, He was the reminder of something else. How clearly we see in John's gospel that Jesus did not see the attractiveness He had for the others as referring ultimately to Himself, but to the Father; the attraction was to Himself, but so that He could lead people to the Father, as awareness and obedience!

In this sense, faith in Christ surpasses and clarifies the world's religious sense. Faith reveals the object of man's religious sense, the object that reason could not reach.

Reason cannot understand all that Christ says, because Christ reveals, unveils what is new and unimaginable, and He does this only once people are bound to him. "He came to that place and He worked few miracles there." Why? "Because they were people with little faith."[28] He found little faith. So, where people don't listen, it's useless to talk. Faith in Christ, as it appears clearly at the birth of the Christian fact, is knowing a Presence as something exceptional, being struck by it and then adhering to what He says of Himself. It is a fact; it is a fact that made it possible for Christianity to erupt into the world. Now we want nothing else but to know and live what happened, as Laurence the Hermit said all that time ago in the early Middle Ages, when he summarized the meaning and the style of his life in these terms, "Then I understood that the whole of my life would be spent in realizing what had happened; and Your 'word' fills me with silence."

Faith is recognizing an exceptional Presence, being struck, coming to be struck by It, a Presence that cannot be compared with other occasions already lived and therefore possible in the future, and adhering to what that Presence tells you about Himself, because if you were not to adhere to what He says of Himself, there would be a contradiction with the judgment you made that what you have met is exceptional, that you were forced to accept as exceptional. So, faith is an act that has reason as its starting point – reason evidently understood not as the capacity to describe God, to talk about God, by substituting for what we call Revelation, but reason as the affirmation that the Mystery is a reality that exists, without which man cannot begin to look reasonably at reality. In other words, the starting point for faith is reason as awareness of reality, that is man's religious sense.

Faith is a judgment, not an emotion. Faith is not a changing feeling that identifies the existence of God as it wants and lives religiosity as it likes. It's a judgment that affirms a reality – a present Mystery.

So, faith is rational, since it flourishes at the extreme boundary of the dynamics of reason like a flower of grace to which man adheres with his freedom. Now how can man adhere with his freedom to this flower that cannot be understood as to its origin and manufacture? For man, adhering with your own freedom means recognizing with simplicity what his reason perceives as being exceptional, with that immediate certainty, as happens with the unassailable and indestructible evidence of factors and moments of reality, as they enter the horizon of your own person. It is a phenomenon that is part of the dynamics of man. Becoming aware of and getting to know reality has many different ways of reaching its fulfilment, depending on the relationships that are established. A true judgment is born of simplicity of heart. The event is experienced at once as being exceptional because it is exceptional, but in order to grasp it in its newness, reason has to accept it at once with simplicity and recognize what happens, and what has happened with the immediate certainty that one has towards any evidence of reality. For before everything else, before the judgment that John gives about that Man, that Peter gives about that Man, before their judgment and adherence, first of all there is this simplicity, this simple heart, these simple eyes, this tension, this simple desire that is open to assimilate, that is able to assimilate with clarity what it has encountered, that aspect of reality that it has come across.

Cardinal Ratzinger, the great defender of the faith in these evil times, wrote:

> By no means the least important practical function of faith is to offer healing for the reason as reason, not to overpower it or to remain outside it, but in fact to bring it to itself again. Faith, as a historical instrument, can set reason itself free again, so that – now that faith has set it on the right path again – reason can once more see properly for itself. [...] Without faith, philosophy cannot be whole, but faith without reason cannot be human. [...] Why has faith still any chance at all?

Because young persons who believe, culturally mature persons who believe, cannot fail to make people speak like this. "I should say," Cardinal Ratzinger continues, "it is because it corresponds to the nature of man. [...] The longing for the infinite is alive and unquenchable within man. None of the attempted answers will do; only the God who Himself became finite in order to tear open our finitude and lead us out into the wide spaces of his infinity, only He corresponds to the question of our being."[29]

In the modern era, by losing the true nature of reason, rationalism makes *confusion between religious sense and faith* quite habitual, thus emptying faith of its true nature. This is the theme that best indicates the origin and synthetizes more the documentation of all the sickness our modern world is living from the point of view of relationship with God and of the religious history of mankind. Modern rationalism, the rationalism of the modern world, that presents itself to man today, to society today, as the privileged criterion, makes the confusion between religious sense and faith something normal, denying its very nature, that is a judgment that involves freedom: affectivity complements the content of this judgment.

The confusion between religious sense and faith makes everything confused. The collapse of faith in its true nature, as it is in tradition, that is, in the life of the Church, the collapse of faith as recognition of "Christ all and in all," as identification with Christ, and imitation of Christ, has given rise to the present-day bewilderment, which reveals itself in various, identifiable aspects. We will describe in detail these typical consequences that, as they are characteristic of the present-day unease, may describe some difficulties and imprecision of our own.

2. A Faith Emptied Out:
The "Five Withouts" of Modern Rationalism

a) The first consequence of rationalism can be summarized in the formula: "God without Christ." It is the denial of the fact that it is only through Christ that God be revealed to us for what He is, that the Mystery reveal Himself for what He is. "God without Christ," or fideism. This is what characterizes all the positions that, by eliminating the reasonability of faith, presume to define God as the idolatry of a particular, felt or inherited from a particular ethnic or cultural tradition, or fixed by one's own imagination or thinking. Fideism empties the foundation of all our religious application, all the Christian conversion of our life, of our life's whole sense of God, of all our moral effort.

b) The second consequence is "Christ without the Church." If the first aspect was identifiable with fideism, the second aspect, that is the immediate consequence of this, is called gnosis, or Gnosticism, in all its aspects or versions.

If you eliminate from Christ the fact of being a man, a real, historical man, then the possibility of a Christian experience made of time and space is also eliminated. A Christian experience is a human experience, so it is made of time and space just like every reality that is also material. If this aspect of the materiality of the object is lacking from the experience that man has of Christ, then the possibility of Christ's contemporaneity is also lacking, that is the truth of what He said of Himself. Therefore, in an ambit rationalistically influenced, the whole of reality made of time and space is scorned as the place that gives rise to the experience of man's ultimate meaning: man's ultimate meaning is not part of day-to-day experience.

You cannot think of Christ without such a concreteness; it would be a reduction and a transformation of what Christ said about Himself, of what Christ is, as the revealer, in the hands of God. Tertullian affirms, "*Caro cardo salutis*" (The flesh is the hinge of salvation).[30] The introduction and the pivot of salvation is in the flesh. God enters into human experience in Christ. *Caro cardo salutis* means that if the hinge of salvation is in the flesh, if the introduction and the pivot of redemption is in the flesh (Christ who dies and rises again), then God, as Christ, as Christ's nature, since in His own nature He took over Jesus of Nazareth, God enters into human experience: it is God who enters with Christ into human experience.

The elimination of carnality, which is implied in every human experience, even in Christ's own experience, draws Christ and the Church back into an abstraction, reducing Him to one of the many religious models. Again, it is Ratzinger who writes:

> The identification of one single historical figure, Jesus of Nazareth, with 'reality' itself, ['reality' is Being, so here it's a question of identifying Jesus of Nazareth with the Mystery, with the origin of reality itself], with the living God, was now rejected as a relapse into myth; Jesus was consciously relativized, reduced to one religious genius among others. There can be no absolute entity in itself, or absolute person in himself, within history, only patterns, only ideal figures, which direct our attention toward the wholly other, which in history cannot in fact be comprehended in itself.[31]

Rationalism dogmatically sustains that Christ God, as such, cannot be grasped in man's materiality, in other words, in history, whose flow is led by the Mystery.

The present-day world's incapacity to accept Christianity lies exactly in this negation: Jesus cannot be God because we cannot speak of a God who becomes man. This is the elimination of Christianity, that cannot survive in an interpretation that would limit the nature and consequences of this enormous affirmation: God has become man. This is why "Jesus" is the invocation that simple people, the common people in their simplicity quite happily recognize. They call on Jesus. If we don't remember, though, that Jesus is Christ, the Son of God, the consecrated man, destined by nature, by his origin, to be part of the Mystery of God, then the invocation, "Jesus," or the affection for Jesus, becomes empty. Jesus as man does not become a place of attraction, an attraction that opens in an unimaginable and inconceivable way to the Infinite. Peter's "Yes" is the opposite. Peter's "Yes" is based on this attraction and affection that Jesus in His flesh aroused. He was a man whom John and Andrew were impressed by.

St Bernard said, "What by nature (Jesus) knew from eternity, He learned through human experience."[32] This quotation clearly sums up Jesus, "God made man." That which by His divine nature, Christ knew from eternity, He learned through human experience. So, it is from Jesus' human experience that we have to start off in order to reach where He wanted to lead us, to His obedience to the Father and to His way of looking at and valuing things, to His way of affirming beauty and goodness, because as the book of Ecclesiasticus says, "God loves what He has created, He made everything He created good."[33] Starting off from the human experience of Jesus, we can reach an imitation of Christ as obedience to the Father, obedience to the Mystery.

c) The third aspect of the effect that the rationalistic world has brought into our ecclesial life, both individual and collective, is "a Church without the world." This is where clericalism and spiritualism come from, as a twofold reduction of the value of the Church as the Body of Christ.

Christian religious life comes to be determined by statism which, unilaterally, is called clericalism. Christian religiosity develops in an environment of rules conceived in a legalistic way (pharisaism); we have practically become agents of a power (either civil, political, or religious). In Jesus' time they were the Pharisees (religious power) and the Romans (political power), today the *pax romana* takes on new forms and bears the names of other nations. However, just as in those days, today all religions are acceptable, provided they imply adoration of the emperor, adoration of the power that is in government.

This is why we feel as our own all the irony with which Péguy is able to talk of the truth that he is living, that he tries to come to terms with:

> So we navigate constantly between two parish priests, we manoeuvre between two gangs of parish priests: the lay 'parish-priests' and the ecclesiastical parish priests; the anti-clerical clerical parish priests and the clerical clerical parish-priests; the lay 'parish-priests' who deny the eternity of the temporal, from within the temporal; and the ecclesiastical parish-priests who want to undo, to disengage the temporal from the eternal, from within the eternal. Thus neither one nor the other are in fact Christians, since the very method of Christianity, the mechanism of its mysticism, of Christian mysticism, is the link between one piece of the mechanism and the other; it is this linkage between two pieces, this singular linkage, this mutual, reciprocal unique linkage that cannot be undone: it is indissoluble; [of the one and the other] of the one in the other, of the temporal in the eternal and (this most of all, what is more often denied, and that in effect is the most wonderful thing) of the eternal in the temporal.[34]

"Church without world!" Augustine, though, says "*Reconciliatus mundus Ecclesia*,"[35] the Church is the world reconciled with God. In order that the world be reconciled, the mystery of Christ in his temporal presence has to enter actively in the world in all its aspects, just as the resurrection of Christ implied the salvation of all the factors of what is human. Christ's resurrection is not salvation unless of man as such, of the whole man.

Spiritualism is faith set alongside life; therefore, faith is no longer the reason that enlightens and the strength that works in life. Every kind of spiritualism has to speak of Christ's resurrection in a sentimental way: the devotion of a remembrance, not the memory of a presence. Thus, Christ is not risen in his body, really: the resurrection is not something present, salvation has not already begun (in such a way that the present life is the development of a seed that is the risen Christ). The sentimental, devotional way in which Christ's resurrection is treated, to which Christ's resurrection is reduced, is the most serious and conspicuous symptom of the spiritualism in its incidence on the people and on the Church as a whole. If the resurrection is not present, then salvation cannot be present, and Christ's resurrection would be like a point that speaks about the future, an unknown future, that last unknown future, reserved to the last step of history.

This is why it is right to say, with Péguy:

> Materialism has its own mysticism, but it is a mysticism that is not at all dangerous. [...] It is incapable of offending because it is so vulgar. [...] The opposite type of mysticism, though, that which denies the temporality of the eternal, is quite different – it seems to be more properly anti-christian. [...] To deny heaven is almost certainly not dangerous. It is a heresy with no future. To deny the earth, though, is tempting. First of all, it is no small thing. Which is worse. [...] Thus, one arrives at vague spiritualisms, idealisms, immaterialisms, religiosisms, pantheisms and philosophisms which are so dangerous precisely because they are not vulgar. [...] To deny temporality, matter, vulgarity, impurity, to deny these, to reject temporality, this is the aim of all aims, this is what is pure, purity, sublime purity.[36]

Salvation is thus conceived eschatologically, only on the last day. In this way man's salvation, as it is defined by the faith, is emptied, because the faith proclaims, tends to bring about, and as far as is possible does bring about, the salvation of the present. Keeping back salvation for the last day in fact destroys the reasonability of the faith, that is, its the humanity and the human concreteness of our relationship with Christ, and, in the end, destroys the very reason for the Church in the world, the identity of the Christian in the world. This would make of the Church not the protagonist, but the courtesan of cultural, social, and political history. The individual Christian would live not a belonging, but an affiliation for the purpose of censuses and voluntary work, in other words, the standardization that we have always spoken of.

This cancels out the fact that Christianity is the proclamation of a profoundly new reality, that involves the whole nature of human reality, but with a further resolution at a higher level, a level not foreseen nor foreseeable, nor discernible, and therefore not immediately feasible for normal human awareness. Christian ontology is destroyed by ethics; just as, for example, in the traditional faith, the conception of a political dimension separated from Christian religiosity has been turned upside down. The ontology of the Christian discourse is destroyed by ethics, because ethics, as awareness and use of reality, develops its line from a concept of what man is, from an idea of what man is that is not touched by the Christian message (as it appears today the conception of a political dimension separated from Christian religiosity). Just as man's nature is saved by something that is greater than man – in which man is whole, humanity is whole, but which carries the power of a subject incomparably greater, infinitely greater – analogically the moral conception, born as it is as the application of an ontology, is saved by Christian ontology, by the ontology proper to the Christian discourse, because the Christian discourse brought by Christ is a different way of thinking, conceiving, and living reality. The ethics which derives from naturalism, from rationalism, becomes destructive towards the ethics that is born, that springs from the ontology of Christian discourse, from the Christian discourse which is the announcement of a new being, a being that is the new humanity, a new humanity.

This destruction leads to statism, in its version of clericalism, as Péguy writes:

> Those who take their distance from the world, those who take on height by leaving the world, leaving the world while debasing the world, don't elevate themselves. [...] Because they do not have the strength and the grace to be of nature, they believe they are of grace. [...] Because they do not have temporal courage, they believe they have begun to penetrate the eternal. Because they do not have the courage to be of the world, they believe they are of God. Because they do not have the courage to belong to one of the parties of humanity, they believe they belong to the party of God. Because they love no one, they believe they love God.[37]

d) From "a Church without world," to "a world without 'I'": this is the fourth "without" in which we gather the reflections we are making at today's situation, the world's situation. As we have seen, the Church without world becomes a clericalism – the impressive effect of fixed laws controlling every detail of life, which tend to describe the attitude to have in every detail of life, in such a way as to cover every possible aspect of human experience, as we see happening today – either a spiritualism – for Church without world means Church, Body of Christ, and Christ without the daily version in which the human I comes to take shape: in this sense, it remains an abstract Church or an abstract conception of life. If the Church is without the world, then this world tends to be without an I: in other words, it is an *alienation*. This world is characterized by alienation as the end result, whether foreseen or not, whether wanted or not – normally wanted by the power, by whoever has the cultural power in that moment.

Briefly, then, the world would be nothing but the ambit of existence defined by the power and its laws; whereas the world is really the ambit in which Christ brings about in time the redemption of man and of history. For rationalist indifference and its antithesis, the world is just reduced to the ambit of existence defined by the power and its laws, which become instruments of violence. A few years ago, there was a magistrate who wrote an article exalting the principle of law and order as absolute, saying that Christmas shouldn't have Christ as its object, but rather law and order, as defined by the state. This reminds me of a phrase of Miłosz that we have often reflected on: "Man has been given to understand that he lives only by grace of those in power. Let him therefore busy himself sipping coffee, catching butterflies. Who cares for the Republic will have his right hand cut off."[38]

The evident and ultimate consequence of this is the loss of freedom. An existence defined by the power and its laws has as its ultimate consequence the loss of freedom, the non-recognition or the abolition of freedom, an abolition not proclaimed theoretically, but in effect put in operation. Then since freedom, however you like to define it, is the face of the human I, it amounts to losing the human person. In fact, it is called alienation.

The "world steeped in lies," is the one that Jesus said he wasn't praying for. Jesus could not pray for the world as a creature awaiting salvation;[39] he spoke of not praying for the "world"[40] in so far as it is dominated by, or lets itself be dominated by another conception, in so far as it is invaded by falsity. Let's recall another phrase of Christ's, "When the Son of Man comes, will he find faith on earth?"[41] This world is the negative, alienating world, where the I is denied and alienated, the world where the meaning of life, time, space, work, affection, society, are not drawn from our belonging to Christ, through our belonging to the Church, but from another culture that draws its beginnings, seeking to develop them to the point of determining their ultimate end, from a naturality that leaves aside (because "it's too difficult") or disputes (because "it's not clear" or because it wants to be free in the instinctive sense) the Mystery of God made man, His happening in the present. This naturality is in force, prevails in the cultural environment we live in.

It is the belonging, not to the society, nor to the state, but to Christ in his Church; it is the belonging to Christ through the belonging to his Church, that is also the origin of political method when it calls itself, or wants to call itself Christian.

e) This I, this alienated I, is "an I without God." The I without God is an I that cannot avoid boredom and nausea. So, we let ourselves go on living: we can feel ourselves part of a whole (pantheism), or else fall prey to desperation (the prevalence of evil: nihilism).

"Nothing is further from me," says Claudel, "than the pantheistic conception, the idea of being, as it were, drowned in a world in which we dissolve ourselves voluptuously [it seems like the definition of the New Age]. This conception has always seemed foreign to me; I have a very strong sense of my personality, of the fact that I am not made to be swallowed up in a togetherness, but, on the contrary, to dominate it and to grasp the meaning it might have."[42]

3. A New Morality

These five aspects of modern-day bewilderment that we have outlined, which originated in the collapse of faith in its true nature, explain, or rather should clarify our own way of behaving; they become well motivated topics for an examination of conscience ("Be ready to give an explanation to anyone who asks you for a reason for your hope").[43]

We have seen what faith in Christ tells us as to how to observe the world in which we are living, and how to win back our freedom in this world, in order to become once again capable of clarity and self-consistency. For the consequences of the situation in which we find ourselves are bitter. This is why I have summarized the five aspects with examples: God without Christ; Christ without the Church; the Church without the world; the world without the I; the I without God. Now we'd like to see, to touch briefly on how the faith in Christ produces not only a new mentality, but also a new morality.

"My just man lives by faith,"[44] says the Holy Scripture. How does the faith as a source of moral laws, give rise to a new morality? How is a new morality born from a belonging to Christ lived in the Church? The world is quite happy to use the word "justice" to identify morality. It's easy for all of us to be tempted to do this, where, by justice, what is really meant is a set of values set out at our own convenience. The new morality that springs from the Christian event is the loving acknowledgment of a Presence linked with destiny. Then as you mature, by remaining in it, you understand that this Presence is continuous. The new morality is the loving acknowledgment of a Presence linked with destiny that continues in history. The whole of previous history reinforces this evidence, because it is evidence! Peter's "Yes" arises and takes flesh from an evidence.

In this sense it is the word "charity" that defines the Christian conception of justice. The true value of the person, its correspondence with Being, is ultimately defined in charity. If a wife deals with her husband without having this perspective, at least implicitly, she cannot treat him well; if a child looks at his parents without this implication, his relationship with them will not go well. It is charity as correspondence with Being: looking at the other person as the term of the relationship conceived as corresponding to Being, and the other person's subject as correspondence to Being. Like when Jesus said to Judas, "My friend, are you betraying me with a kiss?":[45] this is God's justice. This is part of the Mystery. Charity and justice coincide. In the Mystery they are one and the same thing, although the two words are both true in their own way.

God's justice, though, is not man's justice (just as Jesus' charity is different from human charity): it brings about a change. God's justice, recognized, in charity, as the supreme expression of God's attitude towards man and man's attitude towards God, brings about a change, and makes it radical, that is, it goes to the very root of the heart. "Man sees the appearances but the Lord looks into the heart."[46] His justice doesn't close or imprison in appearances. God's justice is always a change of the heart's original, constitutive needs in their totality, that is to say, up to the point of happiness and perfection.

What provoked Peter to say "Yes" is Christ's charity, which changed Peter's remorse at his betrayal into positive sorrow. The remorse of betrayal was transfixed by Christ's charity, and the change to positive sorrow is charity as echoed in Peter; echoed in the sense that Peter accepts it, it is put into action by him, perhaps without even a thought. Peter's "Yes" is the greatest expression of Christ's redeeming work for man. It is the explosion of the positivity of Being over the negativity of the falsehood of man's action.

For this reason, the change that shows the presence of Christ is called witness. It is the work of the I as the work of God, *opus Dei*, according to the freedom that God requires; it has to do with life, time and space, love, work, and society: it is not a suppression of these things, of something of the I in its being, but the ultimate positivity of the whole I in its being.

The change is a fruit of the Mystery in time, of God's plan. Man's task in this is to beg. These are the factors of God's plan. Man's freedom is entrusted with the task of begging, because the power is all God's. "God is all in all" – He created nature, He shared His Being with a creature who, like Christ, was to be the reflection, the splendor, the awareness of what the Father is, the full acknowledgment of the Father. Thus, begging is the expression of the full acknowledgment that man makes of his dependence on God, his acknowledgment of what God is.

The great objection is that Christianity does not keep its promise. In the *Angelus* we answer the invitation of the one leading the prayer when we say, "That we may be made worthy of the promises of Christ." Christ's promise is: "*Mecum eris in paradiso*" (You will be with me in Paradise),[47] as He says to the robber who was crucified with Him, and "the hundred-fold in this world,"[48] as He had said earlier. The objection is born from another aspect of our consciousness, from the fear of sacrifice. Eliot writes, "I believe the season of birth is the season of sacrifice."[49] For the mother and for what she creates, the season of birth is a sacrifice. To evolve the affection you have for a person towards the truth, is a sacrifice. It's a sacrifice not to make money by cheating and subterfuge. It's a sacrifice for a magistrate to keep in mind the person when he is looking for evidence in a criminal case, most of all when he has to decide how to advise the authorities on what steps to take, because a magistrate cannot favour a tendency that would massacre the hopes of a people. Mauriac observed, "The cross [sacrifice] opposes the life [...] as we dream it to be, but the cross is not opposed to life as it is";[50] sacrifice is opposed to the dreams we have, not to life as it actually is.

Sacrifice is the condition for true possession. Time that passes does not cancel, but rather deepens the truth of our possession of everything, in every relationship: nothing is an objection any longer. For if God has become man and has died on a cross for me, where can I find the objection?

The fading of the sacrifice gives place to a more beautiful image. Like in a film when there is a scene that, at a certain point in the story, changes the scene of the moment: it changes in the same scene, but it becomes clearer through a fading process. While the fading is in progress you wait with bated breath, but then you have another scene in which the previous one has become more beautiful. As we have meditated on many times, this is the meaning of "My Youth,"[51] a poem by the Italian writer Ada Negri, who, through the maturing of her experience of faith, as an old woman of seventy, taught us, showed us how the mystery of Being implies this conversion of the concept of sacrifice, of the attitude towards sacrifice. The mystery of Being, which is realized in this valuing of sacrifice more than in any other situation or attitude, is the confirmation of the positivity of everything that man has before him. We feel that the best expression of this is re-born in us when we read Psalm 8:

> O Lord, our Lord, how great is your name through all the earth!
> You have set your majesty above the heavens!
> Out of the mouths of babes and infants you have drawn a
>   defence against your foes, to silence enemy and avenger.
> When I see your heavens, the work of your fingers, the moon and
>   stars that you set in place –
> What are humans that you are mindful of them, mere mortals
>   that you care for them?
> Yet you have made them little less than a god, crowned them
>   with glory and honour.
> You have given them rule over the works of your hands, put all
>   things at their feet:
> All sheep and oxen, even the beasts of the field,
> The birds of the air, the fish of the sea, and whatever swims the
>   paths of the seas.[52]

Man is nothing if he becomes aware of his relationship with Being. He is nothing, yet God has made him, he feels that he is made, he knows that he is made, built, for something great ("With glory and honor you crowned him, gave him power over the works of your hands"). The proof, the sign that man has been crowned with glory and honour, not deserving it from the ontological point of view, is that You, Lord, "gave him power over the works of your hands," over the whole of creation: science, all science, every level of science and of power depends on this. "How great is your name, O Lord our God, in all the earth."

Without the positivity, the indomitable, unsleeping, irreducible creativity that in every moment, before any difficulty whatsoever, finds its origin, its source in the reality of Christ present in his Church, we cannot live. Let's ask this inexhaustible mercy who is Christ, to be able to renew our awareness of the gratitude we owe to Christ, of the gratitude we owe to the Church, our mother, but most of all of the complete surrender to God, of that complete surrender that makes us say at night prayer: *"In pace in idipsum dormiam et requiescam"* (lie down to rest and sleep),[53] in Him as Mystery, in Him as God, in Christ as God, in God a complete surrender. It is man's last possible breath. In Him in peace I relax until I fall asleep, until I surrender myself to sleep. Paradoxically, it is in sleep that man finds the image of his existing, the awareness of his existing for the human glory of Christ in history. May we live this surrender to the Mystery, to Christ, to the Mystery that revealed Itself in that man, in our activities, and may we be filled with wonder so as to feel St Peter's "Yes" (Yes, Lord, I love you)[54] emerging from the bottom of our hearts. This attitude is the marvelous novelty that a Christian must give proof of everywhere he goes, for the human glory of Christ in history. The more this change is seen, the more glory will be given to Christ, the glory of Christ in history will be discovered, wanted, consciously loved above everything else. As a friend told me this morning, the glory of Christ can really become the passion for a young person or for a man.

ASSEMBLY

STEFANO ALBERTO (FR PINO): The work done in the assemblies in the hotels revealed something very significant: the content of the two lessons had an immediate and profound effect on the life of each one of us. The sign of this is the huge number of questions that arrived, but I would like to say, the quality of the questions, too, questions that refer precisely to the key points in the lessons. We have chosen four of them that we would like to put to you.

LUIGI GIUSSANI: Fine.

CESANA: It seems from what you said, Don Giussani, that it is no longer the time simply to do things, or to belong in a formal way: what do you mean by this insistence on change as a change in knowledge?

GIUSSANI: You can understand if you think of the fact that the change is of the I, of my person, of your person, person understood in the totality of its relationships, of its capacity of a relationship with everything, with heaven and earth, with good times and bad times, with friends and enemies, when you get on with your wife and when you are angry with her. The change is of an I that is responsible: in variable degrees, but always responsible. Now this change, precisely because it is a change in the I, begins in your knowledge. Because the I in order to act and to cause to act, starts off from rational motives, even though these rational motives and principles are more often than not implied, implicit rather than explicit and critically aware. This is why Jesus said, referring to those who were killing him, crucifying him, "Father, forgive them, they know not what they do."[55]

Change can be understood also as a circumstance of life; in fact, we tend to conceive the change of our I and of our life as a change in the circumstances in which we live. It is true that change always implies circumstances, but the true change is in our commitment with these circumstances, with the kind of change that takes place in our attitude towards the circumstances. So since it is precisely a change in the I, change cannot but begin from a new knowledge. The change in the I depends on a new knowledge into which the I plunges, into which it is introduced. Yesterday, for example, we spoke of appearances. Change means, can mean, a way of being struck in a different way by appearances. Faced with appearances man can react in different ways; he can think, "This is what it appears to be" – it is the fundamental error that men make – or he can say, "This is not simply what it appears to be." Here it is a question of a change in the conception of things, precisely in the way of conceiving.

So, when Jesus (as a vicar of Milan said in the seminary forty years ago), said to the Father, "Father, forgive them, for they don't know what they are doing," He was building their defence in the narrow margin of their ignorance, the defence of the weakness of those men, the limitation of those men who were killing him. This was the opportunity for the Lord, the Father, to make of their action the beginning of the mystery of the Church.

Without knowledge there is no experience, the human level of living is lacking (because experience is precisely and definitively the human level of living), and so there is no change in man. The circumstances could be made to change for everyone, God could make use of everyone, but in the I that is responsible God cannot fail to use, as his instrument for the change, an experience that is in some way new: an experience. So the whole educative method of our movement, that strives as much as possible to imitate the method that Jesus Himself used for building the Church, is that of introducing us into an experience. If we are not introduced into an experience, a real change is impossible.

FR PINO: I think that it is interesting and important to stress this aspect of the beginning of the change in knowledge. One question in particular came up very often. At one point yesterday, you said that one of the most striking consequences of the modern mentality, of modern rationalism is the confusing of religious sense with faith. Could you help us to understand this aspect better?

GIUSSANI: If man is not awakened to an awareness of himself, if he is not educated, provoked and educated to an awareness of himself, if therefore he is not himself, then he is left a prey to instinctive inputs, to reactions, to a reactivity in which what predominates is the animal aspect. Rationalism tends to conceive reason as the locus of the truth: the truth is what reason allows (where allowing is much more what we have said earlier than even necessarily a judgment), and so it ends up idealizing what it feels. We always end up tending to idealize what we feel, or even more, identifying the truth with what we feel. The religious sense thus comes to be identified with a feeling: it is a feeling, vague or clear, but it is a feeling, not a reason, it has no particular reasons, that is to say, it is not a reality that one reaches as knowledge, leaving behind the first, more instinctive, more mechanical steps.

The religious sense for its part is not a feeling, it is not a bundle of feelings. So it has to do with reason. The religious sense is originally at the beginnings of reason's life, that is to say, man's conscious life. It is there at the beginnings: it is implicit in its being identified with man's very nature. The religious sense is not a feeling and reason is not an activity foreign to it.

Now, faith is acknowledging a Presence. By now we are used to saying it: faith is the acknowledgment of a Presence, an exceptional

Presence. Faith is the acknowledgment of a Presence. This is not a feeling – though it does involve a lot of feeling – it cannot be defined as feeling. The Presence has to do with the eyes, the emotion it generates: it has to do with the eyes, the heart as regards what you feel; but an evaluation of this, the most important evaluation, the evaluation most decisive for all the rest of your life, the whole expression of life, the definition of the acknowledgment of a Presence belongs to that original stage of human awareness, which causes even a child, before a wonder of nature to say, "How lovely!" When he says, "How lovely!" he is expressing not his way of feeling, but a way of behaving that is rational, it is the beginning of a life, a rational journey.

CESANA: As Fr Pino quite rightly said at the beginning, many of the questions that came touched on almost all the points. However, certainly the most frequent were on the question of sacrifice, revealing that whatever we say, we actually still feel the ethical problem. We have chosen a formulation of this question that Fr Pino will read now, and which seems to define the problem best.

FR PINO: The last point of Saturday morning's lesson recalled belonging to the movement. What does belonging mean in day-to-day life? Fear at promises not kept seems to emerge. How can we help each other to overcome this fear? In this sense, what does it mean that the sacrifice is the condition for overcoming this fear?

GIUSSANI: This is the word that most interests and determines our moods or our impressions and the definitions of our movement: it is the sacrifice that is made by inserting your life into the reality of a companionship – the family, by nature, or a human companionship – because the family and a human companionship indicate something Other as the condition for life. This is why we have said that "there is no greater sacrifice than to give your life for the work of Another."

"To give your life for the work of Another" is a great sacrifice, the greatest sacrifice. But, hearing this, something else immediately comes to mind: if, essentially, sacrifice is giving one's life for the work of Another, then sacrifice is an act of love. Because this is what love is: giving one's life for the work of Another is love. Sacrifice is an act of love, in that it is an affirmation of the positiveness of all life, both as an acknowledgment of the supreme Being, and in putting into action the recognition of one's life as reflected on the whole universe. Living one's life as reflected on the whole universe requires an act of love: conceiving all one's own life, one's life as a reflected on the whole universe, as a point of reference of all the inputs that the universe gives to man's awareness, is an act of love, it is the affirmation of Another.

Time and space codify the analogy of this characteristic of existence: space and time codify all difficulties as a positive affirmation of Being. Sacrifice is not the difficulty, but is the starting point from where we can face all our works, our relations with things and with people. Sacrifice, let me insist, is not the difficulty, but the starting point for facing all difficulties, it is, therefore, the positive affirmation of Being. In order to make a sacrifice you need to see, to glimpse a positiveness. Sacrifice for the sake of sacrifice, as a negation, as mutilation, is inconceivable. The fact that most of the time we feel this as prevalent in us, is because we are not aware –

CESANA: – and so we don't make the sacrifice!

GIUSSANI: But one who doesn't make the sacrifice in a relationship doesn't have the relationship in hand, he hasn't begun to live it!

Why does belonging to a movement facilitate the evolution of our awareness, in such a way as to see sacrifice not as a negative phenomenon of living? Belonging to a movement or to a social reality in so far as it concerns life and presumes to decide over life, makes an education possible (a development of man's awareness) to understand that reality, as it prompts or provokes, aims at a positivity: the positivity of Being. Following the charism makes it more feasible to acknowledge this positivity. A charism that starts off, as its origin, from the religious sense realized, made real, fulfilled by the encounter with Christ, makes it more feasible to acknowledge the positivity of everything, everything, even death. Even death: the only possibility, the only chance of death being the extreme positivity of things is given by Being as Mystery. St Paul says it in many pages of his writings, he says it quite off-hand, as if talking about a list of chance events, of case histories, of difficulties and injustices he had to undergo, including death, "whether we live or die, we are the Lord's."[56]

Anyway, the objective factor that the Mystery places in the dynamism of things, the way in which the Mystery communicates the dynamics of everything is precisely sacrifice. Sacrifice when it is lived – and human self-awareness sees this clearly – guarantees the positivity of life, of being, of existing.

"Unless you turn and become like children you will not enter the kingdom of heaven":[57] you will never know and never possess anything. Following the charism makes this invitation of the Gospel actual. Because the way in which the Mystery communicates the dynamics that things have cannot fail to start off from the eyes of a child. A child's way of looking at things starts off from a positive prejudice, not yet developed, not yet fully aware, but it communicates a positivity (a positivity that can immediately lead to a bite, a punch, small wound).

This is why sacrifice is obedience, in the sense that I am not the one who makes reality, what I am I did not make myself, all that is given to me (by the Mystery as from my mother) is the condition for a greater, deeper awareness of everything we do. This is why the sacrifice is obeying, and it starts off from this pre-conception or pre-judice: the datum given, the work of Another.

"*In simplicitate cordis mei laetus obtuli universa*":[58] in the simplicity of my heart I have gladly offered You everything. Offered, as we say in our definition, means that there is no greater sacrifice than giving your life for the Work of Another.

Acknowledging the positivity of being, of everything, as the first intuition or the beginning of an awareness of things you begin to get, is precisely sensing what you will later call obedience: as you get older you understand that it is an obedience. This is why "if you do not become like little children" doesn't mean "unless you become irresponsible or incapable of understanding," but "if you do not become as you were made," in other words, if you do not face up to things, to life as you are made: made by Another, by something Other. So, too the fact that your mother gave you life, and the pain of this life, of the life you have lived does not make you angry in the first place with your mother. The observation about children is really interesting, because all their resistance to pain that breaks out does not cancel their first impact with things: they approach things wide-eyed with all their energy, and when pain hits them, they don't necessarily lose this original simplicity. When they grow up, they complain, but while they are still young, they complain without –

FR PINO: – without complaining.

GIUSSANI: No, they do complain but –

CESANA: – they don't despair.

GIUSSANI: They are not desperate.

FR PINO: There is one last question. We would like you to speak about the glory of Christ: what makes this become the passion of our lives?

GIUSSANI: The true nature of reason is to grasp the being of things, or better, it expresses itself first and foremost as a revision or a seeing and grasping the being of things, things as being. This is the first argument that reason has: the ultimate positivity of the existence of everything is the only definition that justifies man. Reason is made to grasp the being of things: Christ, the supreme moment of creation, "*omnia in ipso constant*"; "in him all things hold together," [59] in whatever way this "all things" be translated.

Christian history tells us this at its origin – adults rather than children: Paul, Peter, the figures of the apostles are not figures of children – they became children again when they saw Jesus – but ethically children, in their attitude towards the people they met; it is in this context that we have been taught this truth, which is the summit of the Christian Mystery in human existence: "Everything consists in Him." It is an assertion that enters our lives in the same way that the reason for the existence of things does: it is an undeniable objectiveness right at the beginning, as we said in *The Religious Sense*.

"If you don't become like little children." If Paul, Peter, James, or John – to speak of those who gave us the first notes of the Christian fact – had not had this childlikeness of spirit, renewed, revived, re-born through the encounter with Christ, if this had not happened to them, they would have given us nothing new. Even in adults, the absolute freshness of the relationship with things gives the impression of a consistency that we cannot deny, which later on becomes complicated, again because of a preconception.

Christ as a reasoning man was conceived by the Mystery as the totalizing moment of the history of the universe, in the time and space of the universe and in the whole history of mankind. Christ is the Sign with which the Mystery coincides totally, really. To refuse Christ is to fall, to become imprisoned in a preconception in the use of things.

To affirm Christ is to affirm objective beauty that gives us a passion for life and everything becomes transparent to our eyes. It is no coincidence that gladness visible on the face is the main argument for Christian witness in the whole world, before everyone. The gladness of your heart, the older you get, as time passes, is the confirmation to ourselves of what we say and what we believe in. But this gladness emerges, can emerge only from an objective beauty, from something that is objectively beautiful and good. Gladness cannot come from something that is not beautiful or good. In this case you could speak of contentment or satisfaction, but not of gladness.

Christ is the Sign with which the Mystery coincides, in reality and in history, in the whole universe and in the history of peoples. This is why to affirm Christ is to affirm something objectively beautiful that gives us a passion for life, and everything becomes transparent to our eyes. Because as long as something, a reality, does not become transparent, begin to be transparent, it is like owning it without owning it, its value remains ambivalent.

Affirming Christ puts us in the first breech from where the Mystery that makes things emerges: what God does, becomes an experience. Christ is the first breech, the first step, He is the first presence: the relationship with Christ makes the whole of life transparent to our eyes. And the verification of this lies precisely in the fact that we become joyful explorers and actors of all that is truly there in things. "I will make known the power of my name by the gladness on their faces."[60] The experience of gladness that our life gives is an absolute positivity, which works in us in the relationship with other men.

"ONLY WONDER LEADS TO KNOWING"

"Ideas create idols, only wonder leads to knowing."[61] This phrase of St Gregory of Nyssa, a great figure of the early Christian centuries, is the same as our conception of getting to know Christ, of acknowledging Christ, which is found in our texts, in our language. How can we define the motivation for saying "Yes" to Christ? The motivation for saying "Yes" to something that comes into our life defeating all preconceptions is beauty: it must imply a beauty and a goodness that we may well not manage to define, but that we can feel as the content of our reason for the gravest decision that our reason has to take: faith. Because faith is born as an acknowledgment made by our reason.

"Ideas create idols, only wonder leads to knowing." The simplicity of children is the truth of our adhering *to* the faith, of adhering *of* our faith to what the Church says, to what the Christian tradition brings us, to what the Church, in the movement, tells us: the childlike attitude, that approaches things without ifs, buts, and maybes, it approaches things, touches them and deals with them, spontaneously. This is why Jesus says, "If you don't become like little children, if you are not like this when you are adults, you will never enter, you will never understand, you will never hear."[62] This is why we, too, say that "ideas create idols, only wonder leads to knowing."

How can we come to acknowledge – we have said in our texts – that we are prompted to adhere to Christ by the movement or by God's Church, by the Catholic Church instead of by other interpretations? "Only wonder": it is the wonder experienced by John and Andrew. This is the word that explains everything that we have said about the beginnings of faith. The act of faith was enucleated, it arose and was developed in John and Andrew (how important for us is this first page of John's Gospel) by a Presence: but it was a suggestive Presence, a striking Presence, an astonishing Presence: "How can He be like this?" It's exactly the same thing that the people we live with may say, may be forced to say, looking at the example of each one of us, at the witness we give, "How can they be so full of gladness?"; "You, how can you be so content?"

The faith – which is the affirmation of a fact, the objectivity of a fact, Christ – gives rise to an aesthetic beauty, in other words a suggestiveness, which reveals an adequate reason really in act: it is an adequate reason that gives rise to aesthetic beauty in a relationship. Because goodness, that is to say, ethics, derives from aesthetics, we say. In so far as the suggestiveness of the figure of Christ struck me as a boy when I joined the seminary – it increased and became more serious later on – this is what forced my hard head or my laziness to look always at the good, to the extent of being aware before God that I do so, or try to do so.

If we do not keep this rule, if we don't try to follow this rule, the goodness, the adherence to morality, to what the Church tells us is morality, it is not persuasive, because it is not a valid proposition for man's nature.

"Ideas create idols, only wonder leads to knowledge," to knowledge, and therefore to conceive of something. Otherwise, one is a victim of preconception: there is no justice in our way of reasoning if it doesn't take account of the preconception from which it is born. Because if we are not like little children, as the Gospel says, we start from a preconception. Therefore, it is impossible to adhere to something that requires a sacrifice on the strength of a preconception: you must adhere on the strength of a force of attraction that it has. Like John and Andrew: "How attractive that Man is!" This is also how the question arose in them, "What is the meaning of what He says of himself? What is He saying about God?"

In our education, then, we need to discover how to perceive, how to bring to the fore and affirm the suggestiveness of a proposal: in this sense, the suggestiveness of a proposal. We take a proposal seriously only if it is suggestive. Otherwise, we take seriously only those aspects of the proposal that we decide on, in other words, we abolish the proposal. The reduction of faith to religious sense happens in this way.

There is no modern philosopher or contemporary artist able to say or think what Gregory of Nyssa said. Today they speak mostly of the emergence of a preference, of a choice in them, putting their own feelings as the only adequate reason, making themselves the starting point in life and in the world.

This is why Jesus used the smallest child as an example to the adults. Because above all we need to be free and true, transparent. Otherwise, an objection arises in everything: all our objections arise from a preconception and build a fortress on preconception: in this way preconception becomes unassailable and prevents any attempt by reason to identify a real truth. Only wonder convinces, that is to say, "leads to knowledge" to the point of conviction, to the point of generating conviction. Preconception really is the elimination of true aesthetics, of the true taste of life.

Christ Is All and in All

(1999)

Giussani's first writings on ecumenism and on the education of young people, collected in a new book (*Porta la speranza. Primi scritti [Bring Hope. First Writings]*), were presented at the Catholic University of Milan by the rector, Adriano Bausola, by Nikolaus Lobkowicz, and by Archbishop Carlo Caffarra. Opportunities to discuss and learn about Fr Giussani's intellectual trajectory seemed to multiply in various places around the world, revealing his contribution to our understanding of human and Christian experience, the method of his thought and his way of relating to modern and contemporary culture. In Buenos Aires, Archbishop José Mario Bergoglio, who had just been named archbishop of the Argentine capital, presented the Spanish edition of *The Religious Sense*. At Georgetown University in Washington, DC, David Schindler and several of his colleagues organized a conference on the thought of Luigi Giussani. In his opening remarks, Stanley Hauerwas expressed that he wished he had written the pages of *The Risk of Education* himself.

After the release of *Fides et ratio*, Fr Giussani wrote a commentary on the encyclical for *la Repubblica*, reflecting back on his first years as a teacher at Liceo Berchet and "the need to make them understand what is meant by reason, because without reason there can be no faith."[1]

A few months earlier, the need to give a more complete form to the long trajectory covered over the last twenty years reached its fulfilment, pulling together reflections, meditations, and speeches in a new book that could be, at the same time, a step of awareness of the journey traveled and that which was still to come. *Traces of Christian Experience* was the name of the booklet Fr Giussani wrote together with his students in 1960, as a reflection on their experience and an indication of the method for being a Christian presence in one's environment, specifically in schools. "New Traces" was the project that would complete the arc, bringing together the development of those first steps and the contributions of a maturity that was reached over the years. Fr Giussani had the idea of making it a collective work, the fruit of an experience in which they matured together, and asked Fr Stefano Alberto and Fr Javier Prades to be coauthors of the book (*Generating Traces in the History of the World*). It was a sign of shared responsibility and, at the same time, an expression of the communal method by which the movement lived and was guided.For the last time, Fr Giussani preached the Fraternity Exercises, still using the tried and tested format of a recorded video. Others would give the meditations in the following years, with a continuity of theme, of sensibility, and of judgment matching the road previously traveled.

In his last letter to John Paul II, in January of 2004, Fr Giussani wrote:

Not only did I have no intention of "founding" anything, but I believe that the genius of the Movement that I saw coming to birth lies in having felt the urgency to proclaim the need to return to the elementary aspects of Christianity, that is to say, the passion of the Christian fact as such in its original elements, and nothing more. Perhaps it was precisely this that awoke the unforeseeable possibility of encounter with personalities of the Jewish, Muslim, Buddhist, Protestant and Orthodox worlds, from the United States to Russia, in an impetus of embrace and appreciation of all that remains of truth, of beauty, of good and of right in whoever lives a sense of belonging.[2]

The profundity of thought found on the following pages documents an attention to the elementary and original components of Christianity, the source which generates the I and the possibility of embracing the other.

Fr Giussani's books, now translated into many languages, have allowed countless people from diverse backgrounds and opinions to encounter that "charism which is a history," and that offers itself to any and everyone as a possibility for life and to build up one's humanity.

Fr Giussani's passion for the unity of the Body of Christ all over the world, which is the Church, sparked during his time at Venegono seminary and matured during the first years of his priesthood, found its surprising confirmation in this renewed and original ecumenical dimension.

––––––––––––

A DECISIVE WORD FOR EXISTENCE

1. The Need for and Evidence of Belonging

"Almighty God, look upon mankind weighed down by its mortal weakness, and bring it back to life through the passion of your Only-begotten Son."[3] This is the point of view by which our heart is moved, and from where it re-commits itself to its baptism.

Last year we said, "Christ is all and in all." Now we must try to understand more deeply, more attentively, with more awareness, what it means, or rather, what must be done for such an evidence – because it is evident for a Christian that "Christ is all and in all" – to become operative in life. We have to read something that God has allowed us to live in our experience, or in that of our brothers too.

For the meaning of "Christ is all and in all" to be clearer to us, we have to recall, too, the method, the phenomenon, the behavioural form that gives rise to a new way of realizing this ideal – which is earthly from one point of view, but eternal as a value. Remember the title we used last year, "The Miracle of a Change." Now in order to change you have to transpose a relationship, cancel it, replace it with another, or you have to deepen the relationship, take it more seriously, try to understand it more, to open yourself more to the communication it makes of itself to us. To this end, the word drawn from the Bible and used by our Christian tradition to say how the miracle of change happens, on one hand is the expression of a condition, and on the other it indicates the power of conversion, power and direction of change: *belonging*. Change, therefore, has belonging as its condition, it stresses the word "belonging" as the decisive one for existence.

But what is meant by belonging? Man becomes aware of his humanity, and therefore uses words to describe it, drawing their meaning from his experience. Man uses his reason, feelings, the inclinations that make up experience and from this he learns. The words man uses throw light on his awareness of the experience they spring from. A well-known psalm, number thirty-two says, "Do not be senseless like horses or mules; with bit and bridle their temper is curbed, else they will not come to you."[4] Man, as we said, wants to be aware, he is forced to be aware of his humanity (in a certain sense he is forced not to be complete, fulfilled or in some way perfected, but to be aware). Man becomes aware of his humanity by observing that experience which is the form in which his humanity is revealed and which constructs man's reality through contact with what he meets. With his reason man has this task of clarifying what he manages to see and grasp in his experience. Otherwise, preconception or pre-fabrication imposes itself.

The love man has for himself makes him aware, or tries to make him aware of what he is. It is because he is reasonable that man seeks to clarify what he is able to look at and grasp in his experience of reality.

In any case, if we don't start off from experience in order to understand ourselves and our reality, it means that life is lived under the influence of preconception or by adopting a prefabricated idea that imposes itself. Let's remember Alexis Carrel's observation quoted at the beginning of *The Religious Sense*, that is as fundamental as it is synthetic, and which says it all, all the objectivity needed, since man reaches objectivity about things more by means of a moral attitude than a debatable intelligence. "Few observations and much discussion are conductive to error: much observation and little discussion to truth."[5] So reason has precisely the task of clarifying what can be seen and grasped.

What does belonging mean, then, for man's experience of self, through which he can truly understand what this word means? The first thing that emerges from an examination of experience is a still unconscious, and then always unaware, evidence of the fact that man *depends*; he has been made. *The Religious Sense* says right at the beginning, in the first chapter, "man truly affirms himself only by accepting reality, so much so that he begins to affirm himself by accepting his existence; accepting, that is, a reality he has not given himself."[6] This is the reason that makes us say that man belongs to God. The same reason pushes this ultimate evidence of dependence on God, as man's dependence on Another, on something Other than himself, to the point of belonging to the instruments that God can make use of, that is to say family and society. This belonging often seems incongruent, for example when one's parents can become non-authoritative and contradictory to the heart of the I. Or, above all, when society usurps a power that tries and presumes to shield man from every other influence that may determine him, even from his own parents. The state is led to regard man as an individual, a factor in function of itself.

In this sense prayers based on the biblical Psalms are truly laudable and comforting. Psalm 139 says, "You formed my inmost being; you knit me in my mother's womb. I praise you, so wonderfully you made me; wonderful are your works! My very self you knew; my bones were not hidden from you, When I was being made in secret, fashioned as in the depths of the earth. Your eyes foresaw my actions; in your book all are written down; my days were shaped, before one came to be."[7] The human I is dependent, and from his experience man discovers the need and the evidence of a total dependence. Just as reason is structurally, naturally, a tendency to grasp reality according to the whole of its factors, by analogy human experience discovers the need and evidence of a total dependence, a dependence that lies at the source of his being as such, an all-embracing dependence. Man cannot fall short of this, otherwise he is distracted and no longer makes use of himself.

The Bible comes to the aid of the feelings that man has of his experience: the words that man finds in his conscious contact with what surrounds him focus his radical belonging to his Creator, and say something inevitable about the human I, about the summit of creation that is the I. It's clear that the I cannot be treated as an insubstantial apparition of the cosmos, but rather according to what Psalm 8 says of him, as the supreme value, the value for which it pleased God to create the cosmos: "What are humans that you are mindful of them, mere mortals that you care for them? Yet you have made them little less than a god, crowned them with glory and honor."[8]

The belonging that is proper to the creature (in the general sense) implies, in actual fact a development that is consciously tangible and perceptible to man. So, change – for the whole of nature, for all creatures, but also for man – is first and foremost a diversity compared with the previous moment, consciously notable by man. The idea of change is dominant in a religious spirit, as for example that of St Augustine, who imagined that God had created the world creating *rationes seminales*,[9] creating the seed of everything, as it were, (that is, basically, quite analogous to the explanation that scientists give of the evolution of the earth and of the cosmos). But it is only for man that an event happens in which the Mystery from which he totally

comes reveals Itself to him in the mystery of Its Being, in His mystery
of Being; so that, in his relationship with Being, with the Mystery of
God, man, who has the power to know Him, also has the power to
act on the whole cosmos as a figure in motion in the imitation of
God. For as Psalm 8 suddenly adds, "You have given them rule over
the works of your hands, put all things at their feet: all sheep and
oxen, even the beasts of the field, the birds of the air, the fish of the
sea, and whatever swims the paths of the seas."[10]

"You have put all things in his hands." Marco Bersanelli's texts in
Traces are a fascinating (although merely suggestive) confirmation
of what Psalm 8 says. Speaking of the cosmos in continuous expan-
sion, there is evidence, now it is impossible not to say it, that this
universe has been made in function of the emergence of the I, so that
there could emerge, in the confused being of things, in the immense,
yet finite cosmos, that point called the I, where the whole cosmos
becomes conscious. The whole cosmos, then, becomes conscious of
itself and understands what it is and what it is destined for, in this
point that is the I, in other words, man. But even the I belongs to
Another, to Him to whom the cosmos belongs.

At this point man's nature throws light on the first decisive consequences of this belonging to God. For example, man's nature is
freedom, because his origin lies totally in Being, in Mystery. The
nature of freedom is precisely to acknowledge this totalizing origin,
that is to say, the totalizing origin of our relationship with God (this
is why I quoted Ps 8). The I is relationship with infinity, there is nothing in between; in other words, it is created, made by the Mystery as
a relationship with the Mystery Itself. Freedom is adhering to Being.
Thus, all the events of creation confirm that man is originated from
"something" that precedes him, something whose possession of reality is incontrovertible, in other words, from the Mystery.

"Man cannot be self-sufficient: that would mean that he did not
exist. In this lies the secret of human existence,"[11] says Berdyaev.
In order to be free, man cannot be self-sufficient: this is the contradictory condition that gives scandal, or the question that nourishes
man's desire to go deeper. But the creature belongs to this Mystery,
so it is certainly not a contradiction: to say that man cannot be self-
sufficient is to say what man's nature is. The mystery of existence lies
in the fact that man exists while not being self-sufficient.

The Mystery is that which lies beyond, above, further off, near or
far as it may be, however it may be imagined. The creature belongs

to this mystery. That the creature belong to the Mystery is not only put in fibrillation by the fact of freedom, because freedom means also the possibility of original expression, creativity, in other words, on man's part. As I see it, this is what clarifies the whole of David's eighth Psalm. Man is greater than every other thing, or better, he is the point in which the vision of the whole cosmos becomes transparent or tends to become so. God could have made the cosmos for just one I. What a huge throng instead, what an endless number of men make the glory of God! Man is great because his relationship with God makes him great. Even though, to our eyes, at the touch of a human hand that would take hold of him, before the demands that society seems to have, what is man? If he gets old, what is man? This type of thought comes to you even as regards children, not only old people. Then you forget childhood and old age as the years pass during which you are totally distracted and drawn by what you are doing or that you think you are doing. But "God is all in all."

2. *The Denial of Belonging and its Consequences*

Man – the concrete man, I, you – once was not, now he is, tomorrow will be no more: so he depends. He either depends on the flow of his temporal ancestors, and is a slave of power, a slave of whoever manages to possess more; or he depends on what lies at the origin of the flow of things, beyond them, in other words, on the divine. Only the divine can save, can put man in a place worthy of Him.

With an extreme sensitivity towards the shore that we feel to be ours, the Jewish writer Hannah Arendt affirms:

Without action, without the capacity to start something new and thus to articulate the new beginning that intervenes in the world with the birth of every human being, man's life, strung out between birth and death, would be truly damned without possibility of salvation [...]. With all its uncertainties, action is like an ever-present *memento* that men, even though they must die, are not born to die, but to give rise to something new. *Initium ut esset homo creatus est*, says St Augustine [man becomes man when he begins something, but man always begins something, as soon as it is born, a creature always begins something; and the development of this beginning is in the hands of God, they are in the hands of Him to whom man belongs]. With the creation of man the principle of starting things entered the world – this is obviously only another way of saying that with the creation of man the principle of freedom made its appearance on earth.[12]

Man becomes man when he begins something; but man always begins something, always: the newborn creature begins something, and the developments of this beginning are in the hands of God, they are in the hands of Him to whom man belongs.

The crowning aspect of modern culture, whether of the right or the left, which has excluded all the recognized presence of the ancient value of yesterday's world, is the abolition of the past, of what came before, therefore the destruction of the value of belonging. In the place of the value of belonging, modern civilization, modern culture places freedom, understood as non-adhering to being as Mystery, thereby constituting a source of falsehood. Jesus says of the devil that he is the "father of lies."

Not adhering to being is the killing of freedom. So modern culture, in affirming man as the measure of all things, in actual fact suppresses freedom, stifles it, because it will not let it be, it cannot let it be, nor conceive it or possess it except as a lie. "Why do you not understand what I am saying?" says Jesus, "Because you cannot bear to hear my word. You belong to your father the devil and you willingly carry out your father's desires. He was a murderer from the beginning and does not stand in truth, because there is no truth in him. When he tells a lie, he speaks in character, because he is a liar and the father of lies."[13]

As well as being a liar, the man of modern-day culture is violent, too: the theoretical denial, but above all the practical denial of our belonging to God is falsehood, a source of falsehood and therefore of *violence*, a violence as long as history, in all the ambits and rela-tionships of society (therefore in the family, too, even in the most extolled friendships, even with those who fight alongside us, who work alongside us). Every human relationship that is not awareness of destiny, that is not therefore awareness of belonging to something Other is violence, too.

This violence reaches the point where it can call itself justice, where the laws aim to solve all the problems of man in society, almost as if man belonged totally to the society he lives in. But the soul, the relationship with God, is not outside the place where man sits in his body, where he eats and meets with his friends, it is not outside it: the soul is not something else, and this has to be said of all man's operating, of all his actions, because his primitive or most powerful concern should be his link with God, his relationship with God.

Today, instead, everyone, even priests and theologians, tend to extol "teaching people to respect the law" as a fundamental value and, while they say things like this, they forget that the laws of man, are always partial, judged by the laws of God. You cannot isolate justice depriving it of all the aspects and factors in which even the verdict of a magistrate can affect a man.

"For they did not keep my ordinances," said Ezekiel, "but despised my statutes [...], with eyes only for the idols of their fathers [they inherited the errors of their fathers]. Therefore, I gave them statutes that were not good, and ordinances through which they could not live."[14]

The power of society, which transforms itself even into laws, must be subject to judgment by another law that is precisely the law of belonging to God; this belonging is all-embracing because all the ephemeral things that participate in the great belonging to God (including the family, the society, the state) can exist only in the comparison that they have with the Eternal, with the eternal law, with the law of God. So, even if they enjoyed an awed condescension from the readers of certain papers, they will not be left in peace by God. There can even be a change that the law seems to guarantee, but it will not be a true one, nor a moral one, because man is not a product of society, and society cannot be interpreted only as an opinion of the state, violently agitated by justice, so that the state poses as the right of power, almost like a divinity.

Violence and slavery. The lack of identity between freedom and belonging, that is to say a freedom not motivated by belonging, forebodes enormous wars.

"I do not like your cold justice; and from the eyes of your judges, gazes always the executioner and his cold steel. Tell me, where is the justice found that is love with seeing eyes? Then invent me the kind of love that not only bears all punishment but also all guilt!" Nietzsche says, oddly, in *Thus Spoke Zarathustra*.[15]

"It's an interesting fact," Arendt intelligently observes, "that the attempt to save human nature at the cost of the human condition should come in a moment in which we all know well [...] the attempts to modify man's nature by radically modifying the traditional conditions. The various experiments carried out by modern science and politics to 'condition' man have no other scope but the transformation of human nature in the name of society."[16] Human nature is identified as order, therefore as power, by society.

"Fools say in their hearts 'there is no God'."[17] This foolishness has become the theory of the world. Thus, we too follow the tide, or can follow the tide, feeling overcome by the wave in which everyone is or seems to be agreed. But it is foolishness! You can put to death everyone in a state who believes in God (as they have done many times with Christians) but you cannot take away God, because He is in the very structure of our consciousness and He is the only source of self-awareness, in virtue of whom self-awareness is a continuous enrichment, can be a continuous event of discovery towards the truth, which never becomes something that we can grasp.

The problem is a radical one, because they are two worlds that confront each other: one that accepts its belonging to God and one that does not accept it. The one who says he does not accept, who actually refuses to feel the jolt of the concept of belonging that we are now stressing, says again that man is the measure of all things. But if man is the measure of all things, forgetting the tragedy that our whole Western civilization is undergoing thanks to its incandescent and unordered self-affirmation, he cannot be discovered except as a denier of belonging; and this denial of belonging as the denial of God tends to become denial of belonging to all the rest (to a company, to a country's history, to a friendship). All the same, man as measure of all things, in order to deny his belonging to God, cannot escape belonging to preconceptions (that can be blocked only in words), which make him act according to non-rational influences, although not consciously.

We say to whoever avoids belonging to God that, without it, there is neither history nor tradition (instead, if belonging to God is acknowledged, it is impossible not to feel what went before, what God brought into existence before us). Thus, there is no more drama for the I, since there is no freedom. For you cannot make a comparison with nothing, or with something useless, or with an abstract morality! As Camus said, "One must encounter love before having encountered ethics. Or else one is torn."[18] But what is love? Love cannot be anything but either the attempt to possess for your own fleeting ends, or companionship on the road, in every case, with no delay, that starts off from a desire for the other's destiny. "Before meeting a morality you have to meet a love" that is to say you need to "re-establish morality through the 'You.'"[19] These two affirmations of Camus are very meaningful and right and come near to our concept of Christian morality, because without saying "Yes" – "Yes" to Jesus – Peter is not tranquil in his morality: his morality would pay its tariff to the temple and to the Israelite context.

Whoever withdraws from belonging to God, then, is estranged from everyone. He's alone, defined moreover by economic and commercial parameters, he lives another, ostensible belonging that does not exist, that is the only position for denying belonging to God: it is the belonging to the world, of which Jesus said, "I do not pray for the world."[20]

"Nothingness," says Arendt again, "becomes a full substitute for reality, because nothingness brings relief. The relief, of course, is unreal; it is merely psychological, a soothing of anxiety and fear."[21]; "When man is robbed of all means of interpreting events, he is left with no sense whatsoever of reality."[22] A regime has this effect.

Thus as Mario Luzi says in an acute expression, "in modern man the solicitations and the invitations of the memory no longer coincide with those of hope, but live independently."[23] Man is invited to something that does not answer to his hope, to the hope he actually has in himself, he immediately does things that are suggested not by his hope, and therefore it is an extraneity that ruins his step.

I want to move on now towards the completion of what I have said, by pointing out the most imposing characteristic in which the Christian conception of belonging to God, of the belonging to the Mystery who makes all things, is translated: it is like a light that must illumine all relationships, so that the relationship be well-proportioned and lived well.

3. The Historicity of Belonging

We belong to the Mystery; we belong to God. But by what road do we go to Him, to the Mystery? If a belonging to the Mystery is acknowledged in us, by what road can we go to meet Him? How can we know the way that He has traced out as the answer to this need for belonging? Because belonging is made of a proposal, an acknowledgment, a bending of our lives to that acknowledgment and to the direct experience of the belonging with the fulcrum indicated. Has the Mystery sketched out some answer to this idea, to this need for belonging? Has the Mystery traced out some road? We belong to the Mystery; and so, by which road does He want us? How can we live this belonging with the Mystery?

Belonging to God implies *historicity* as its essential factor; historicity means persons and things that we know, that we can touch and see; it means things that are ours and, since they are ours, they can be manipulated. Belonging to God implies historicity as its essential factor – here lies the genius of the Creator, who made His Lordship felt in a certain way. This is why He is called Lord. He is the Lord. Let's recall that moment when Moses was talking with God on the mountain, and God passed before him hidden in a cloud, saying "The Lord, the Lord, a merciful and gracious God."[24]

THE CHOICE OF A PEOPLE

The Jews and Christian society both define God clearly as the foundation of the belonging of every I: a belonging that is of every man, even if he is neither Jew nor Christian. But there is a radical difference (even between Jew and Christian).

You cannot speak of belonging to God without grasping, following, and imitating all that He has decided to make man know, because God makes Himself known within history. History is time and space that roll along drawing man towards his destiny.

The whole history of the whole world becomes clear in a current that starts off from a man from Mesopotamia, Abraham. God chose him in order to make Himself known to men and in order to save men who were drifting along in a total forgetfulness, or in an affirmation of the whole according to their own measure. The other religions constitute an interpretation that man gives to the Mystery. Instead, the choice of Abraham is the first moment in which it is possible to receive an interpretation of our relationship with the Mystery, conceived in concrete terms. "God," says the Jewish philosopher Martin Buber, "wants to come to his world, but He wants to come to it through man. This is the mystery of our existence, the superhuman chance of mankind."[25]

Abraham leaves his land out of pure trust in God. To that man God communicates Himself and, in the mystery of His presence to him, two thousand years before Christ, arouses the capacity of a thought, the intuition of a bond with Himself that is in no other part of the world. It is so unthinkable, so inconceivable, that it is difficult to find adequate interpreters. Abraham was the source of this most pure idea of God that the whole history of Israel had.

The centre of this relationship that God establishes with Abraham and his descendants is *election*. Abraham was elected, chosen as father of a new flux, a new people.

The mode of the election, or choice, or privilege, unveils the way, implied in real historical events, that is peculiar to the Mystery's communication of self to man. The Mystery communicates Himself to the man He chooses, to the people He privileges, revealing what He wishes of Himself. One cannot even imagine how to limit God's freedom!

The process of election enters into history with the powerful presumption of being a teaching for the whole world. From the Psalms it can be seen that the Jews, even in Jesus' time, had a passion, a powerful desire to go off on a mission. Their life, the life of their groups, was the instrument of the mission that was to make this God known in the world, a clear idea of whom they had inherited, above all, as total power, as inscrutability ("My ways are not your ways."[26]) and as justice.

The process of election teaches that God makes Himself known through a concrete contingency in time and space (fortunate is that time and space in which God enters: there is no other place in the world so beautiful). The Jews called the place in which God communicated Himself to man and judged them the Temple.

There are no other people in the world that has had such a relationship with God. The other peoples were struck, and drew light from the Jews in order to grasp in their own existence what was already clear there. Thus, the reading of ancient times, of what arose in the past, from the origin of things, places the Jewish man at the centre of the cosmos as regards human awareness. Human awareness was imbued and enriched by the translation into existential terms, into action, of belonging to God, to the God of the Temple, because the way of conceiving the relationship between God and man in Jewish society was the Temple: God gave His advice and His help in the Temple.

"Thus says the Lord: 'Stand beside the earliest roads, ask the pathways of old which is the way to good, and walk it; thus you will find rest for your souls.'"[27] The past is not the past, the past is the formation of the present. "Think back on," says Moses towards the end of his life, "the days of old, reflect on the years of age upon age. Ask your father and he will inform you, ask your elders and they will tell you."[28] But then the whole of modern culture sees belonging as an enemy, because "the elders, the years long past" are words that indicate the mysterious provenance of what stirs us, and, we know, makes us act.

That people have a harder time of it than all the other religious currents, because the unity and the holiness of God, in other words of the Mystery, fall upon each day's doings. The soul, the conscience, perceives this intervention of God, but the body weighs down the soul, the body that decays restricts the breadth of the soul (*"et corpus quod corrumpitur aggravit animam"*).[29] But God, the God of the Bible imposes Himself. God's unity and holiness affect the actions of every day. "Hear, O Israel! The Lord is our God, the Lord alone! Therefore, you shall love the Lord, your God, with all your heart, and with all your soul, and with all your strength. Take to heart these words which I enjoin on you today. Drill them into your children. Speak of them at home and abroad, whether you are busy or at rest. Bind them at your wrist as a sign and let them be as a pendant on your forehead. Write them on the doorposts of your houses and on your gates."[30] This suggests what belonging to the Mystery implies, it means that the Mystery penetrates all our flesh and bones and all we do. God is all in all.

The Mystery's decision to choose a people as the vehicle of His entry into the world, as awareness and operativity, is a *risk* to which the Mystery Himself entrusts Himself in order to deepen and mature the belonging to Him of human existence and to ensure in this way the awareness of the lasting nature of the people's and the individual's belonging to Him, within the contingencies wherein He invests them.

In a word, it is as if the Mystery were to have said, "I want, we want an acknowledgment from nothingness." How can you get an acknowledgment from what is nothing? What should this nothing say to Being? Even the way we are talking of it is imaginative! It is as if the Trinity were to have said, "Let us make something by which we can be acknowledged." It is as if God had decided to say, "Even nothingness is obliged to listen to us and approve us. Nothingness must say, 'I am nothing, but You are.'" And how could God do this, create something of the kind? He made man, the human I, which is freedom. But what is freedom? Freedom is acknowledging Being, adhering to Being. So, not acknowledging Being squeezes the being that He has given us, constricts it, stifles it, weakens it and stupidly, then, from this debilitation, from this contradiction that God and life put before his eyes, man finds a pretext for philosophizing and draws many consequences: it is as if there were a fire in his house and instead of throwing water on the fire, he were to throw the water in the opposite direction.

The Mystery's decision to choose Himself a people is a risk that the Mystery commits Himself to. Time that passes becomes a carrying forward of that history. History is made of events: Abraham, Isaac, Jacob. It is a river, a reality in movement that is born of the initiative of the Mystery, through an historical source, Abraham, and through the leaders of his people after him. So, it is striking that God should make use of a people and that this people claim to have been chosen. (We, too, had to entitle the volume on Christianity *At the Origin of the Christian Claim.*[31]) Event after event, the existence of certain families, certain tribes is asserted, all of them determined by the original position of their ancestor. In the same way as for the previous tribe, they established an ultimate intensity of relationships that were loaded with meaning. All this pivoted on the best known and greatest figure, Moses. At the time of Moses, this history was already so rich in particular factors, that he became the greatest commander, the greatest teacher, the one who evoked the bond with God and the respect and love to have for the place in which the belonging was recalled and in which the earliest signs of the hope with which the people had set off and for which they had accepted the journey could be found.

The Covenant, then, identifies the supreme mode of the relationship between man and God, between the chosen man and God (because the man chosen should make this known to the whole world: to his people and, through his people, to the whole world). Covenant, that begun with the people of the Bible, is brought to completion, to its final realization, in the Christian people. So, someone chosen by God, in order to belong to God, must belong to these people (this is why we said that we too are Jews). "'I am God the Almighty. Walk in my presence and be blameless. Between you and me I will establish my covenant, and I will multiply you exceedingly.' When Abram prostrated himself, God continued to speak to him."[32] No history narrates more dramatic things than these.

"There is no other people that lives on such a footing with their God. They are an old people and they have known him for a long time! They have experienced his great goodness and his cold justice. They have sinned often and repented bitterly, and they know that while they may be punished, they will never be abandoned," says Roth in his book *Wandering Jews.*[33]

"My covenant with you is this: you are to become the father of a host of nations. [...] I will render you exceedingly fertile; I will make nations of you; kings shall stem from you. I will maintain my

covenant with you and your descendants after you throughout the
ages as an everlasting pact, to be your God and the God of your
descendants after you."[34]; "Your God." Yours! You are God's, you
belong to the Mystery, because He made you, completely! God says,
"your God" to one for whom the Mystery is everything: he comes
from God and therefore is God's.

"It was not because you are the largest of all nations that the
LORD set his heart on you and chose you [...] It was because
the Lord loved you and because of his fidelity to the oath he had
sworn to your fathers."[35] This love and this faithfulness last in time.

The word "Covenant" meant the promise of happiness for everyone and the final triumph of God's people over all the nations. So,
the Covenant (in other words, the relationship between God and
his elect) is the fascinating definition of God's behaviour towards
the created world: God wants to save all men that were destined to
death (because this is the reading that all men make of their precarious existence). For without a relationship with God, man is finished.

The Covenant indicates, specifies, how that to which man (and
the cosmos) belongs, God the Creator, stays at his side. "For this
command which I enjoin on you today is not too mysterious and
remote for you. It is not up in the sky, that you should say, 'Who
will go up in the sky to get it for us and tell us of it, that we may
carry it out?' Nor is it across the sea, that you should say, 'Who will
cross the sea to get it for us and tell us of it, that we may carry it
out?' No, it is something very near to you, already in your mouths
and in your hearts; you have only to carry it out."[36] This chapter of
Deuteronomy has always been of great support and comfort.

The Covenant therefore implies:

1) that the whole of mankind belongs to the mystery of God, who
enters into the lives of men engulfed in evil, whom He intends to
save (the evil is original sin, to which men created by Him and whom
He intends to save, give in);

2) that the method of this salvation is to affirm more and more
the value of God through those whom He chooses first so that they
become aware of Him and therefore become missionaries of this in
the world, in order that everyone may become aware of Him. This is
the true, complete, total concept of belonging. (Because there is also
a common denominator of belonging; someone belongs to his dog,
if at night there is no one there apart from the dog, and he hears it
bark, he depends on the dog. But that's rather different!) There is no

human life that does not have this motive, this aim, that should not serve this end: being God's missionaries, because God is Being, He is everything, He is the Being of whom all things are made; and Being means positivity, in the end it is positivity (as it is definitively clear in the idea of mercy of which we have spoken on other occasions).

JESUS OF NAZARETH

At this second point – after hinting at the strange beginning and at the strange conception of the Jewish people as the place pertinent to the presence of God, where the relationship with God could be lived – belongs the birth, in a typical moment of history, of the problem of the Messiah, of Him through whom God was to save man. The prophets called Him the Servant of God.

In the life and the awareness of the Jewish people there was a vacuum: the expectation of how God would make use of them in order to reach other people. God's reply was more powerful than pure knowledge of God, and the incomprehensible, terrible event of original sin: the announcement of a new factor enters the history of man. This is the content of the awareness and the expectation destined to be communicated to the world.

The Covenant remains the inconceivable method that man's heart has as the supreme way for his life and for the faithfulness of the people to the God who is faithful: the faithfulness of the people that will fulfil the promise made by God to Abraham, finally brought into the world by the Messiah, that is, Christ, Jesus of Nazareth. God never asks anything but a re-working of the initial event with a deeper and wider horizon.

Years, millenniums pass and, amidst the whole of the chosen people, that tiny remnant that keeps alive the promise made by the Mystery as the meaning of existence is astounding. Making use particularly of the awareness of the prophets and the ancients, this remnant keeps faith, and is shocked by the fact that a certain flow, a certain stream points out a date as the moment of definition of what God is for them (i.e., "all in all"). At a certain point a date is given. Already some hundred years before Christ the ancients and the prophets were saying that there would be an emissary of God who was to set the people right; and amongst the Hebrews it was a dream attached to the expectation of the Messiah and of the political triumph of the Hebrew people. That stream points to a date as the moment of definition of what God is for them, a date, near the Jerusalem of Herod, and also (in some prophetic spasms) to the name of the town in which the Messiah was to appear.

We cannot fail to apply all this to us! Thirty years ago, a Christian's judgment on the world in the light of its destiny could be fully lived out by his having a morally committed conscience. But not these days: we are called to be fully aware of all the aspects in which the Mystery desires an acknowledgment, through which his divine dignity is delivered from the errors of forgetfulness, corruption, and extraneity, in which the chosen ones, the new tribe or people in the world were floundering, along with other men, feeling discarded and punished for their crimes.

The sense of the Mystery, of the Infinite becomes a different way of behaving in history. It is mercy that acts on the people and on the Covenant with justice (justice is the universe in which God's plan is conceived as being realized in the world and acknowledged by the elect). God cannot fail to sustain man whom He has created in order to have a finite thing, a finite being with whom He shares his own Being, and who acknowledges Him as his Lord. This acknowledgment is what gives the whole creation worth!

The whole human race does not acknowledge God, and thus betrays itself: even though God brought His intentions, his mode of dominion to the surface in a remnant. The Jewish people brings mankind to the awareness that there is an enigmatic evil in man's heart. Original sin goes on, justice seems impossible, but the remnant of Israel cannot look at the beautiful sunset in the evening, or bask in the light of dawn without expecting something, and without knowing it is expecting something.

The Lord, God, the Mystery has answered positively to all this flowering of expectancy, of purified and really devout desire: "I am with you." While others, as we said before, yielded to worldly temptation, God gave a positive answer to this people: Christ. God's answer inserts a novelty into man's vision, a great positivity, even though the people, as such, does not acknowledge Christ in Jesus of Nazareth. A remnant of Israel realizes it, though, on the day when the child is presented to the Father in the Temple: a being generated in a woman, perfectly human, who is to grow and understand what the Mystery has done in Him and with Him. Then He will become greater still and will declare before everyone: "The Father and I are one."[37]

But the presence of Jesus, as the answer to the long expectation of the people and of all peoples, is to last through the whole of history.

We know that the expectation is the expectation of the Redeemer and, therefore, of personal happiness. The expectation of every man is the expectation of the Redeemer. "If this God touches you, it is because it has the face of a man,"[38] Camus says. Jesus of Nazareth, in whose hands the Father has given all things, affirms Himself in history in a mysterious Body, since He assimilates to Himself all those elected, that is all those He chooses in baptism (He is the one who chooses), and makes them part of His body, affirming Himself such where two or three are gathered together in his name: the Body of Christ is there. This unity in all the ages of history is called the new and eternal Covenant.

"The Christian is not defined by a minimum level," says Péguy, "but by communion. You are not Christian because you reach a certain moral, intellectual or even spiritual standard, you are Christian because you are of a particular race [...] a race that is spiritual and carnal, temporal and eternal. Of a particular blood."[39]

IF ONE IS IN CHRIST, HE IS A NEW CREATION

1. The Event of a New Humanity

I'd like to start off by reading two pieces from Giorgio Gaber's *Canzone dell'appartenenza* (*Song of Belonging*) that many of us know. "Belonging is not a casual gathering of persons, it is not an agreement to apparently get together. Belonging is having the others inside you." But how can this "having the others inside you" be realized? (It seems a dream to me.) The last line of the song says, "I would be sure to change my life if I could begin to tell us."[40]

Belonging is the synthesis of the attitude that man must have towards God; and it is a natural evidence that permits the creation of this point of view, that then becomes so useful for our memory. If man belonged to nothing, then he would be nothing. Belonging implies naturally, at least in natural terms, the fact that an I that was not, now is. If man did not belong to anything, in his self-awareness the image of nothingness would be before him, or behind him, when the memory is focused by something else, for a moment or for a few moments. If there weren't the awareness of a belonging, then, if he thinks, if he reflects, he would be faced with his own nothingness.

"He who desires Truth cannot be satisfied with mere nihilism," Pavel Florensky justly observed. "If reason," he continues, "is not associated with being, then being is not associated with reason."[41] The act of knowing is not only gnoseological, but also ontological; it is not only ideal, but also real. If reason does not participate in being, if it does not acknowledge that something before reason imposes itself on it, or rather, if it does not acknowledge that it was made for this further encounter, beyond a self-awareness, it cannot even begin to know. St Thomas really asserted this well when he said that reality, the encounter with reality, immediately arouses the I and that the I is influenced and recalled by reality.

Belonging to God is the most evident thing that a naturally conscious man must admit – must admit, can acknowledge! The most evident thing is this totality of belonging, precisely this belonging to God: man did not exist, and he was made by God, by Another, by something Other, just like the cosmos. Nothing in the cosmos is self-made, there is a precedent that imbues from deep within, and sets everything up: made by and thus belonging to. God is the Creator; creation belongs to the Creator. This is not an image that can be identified with our grasp of things, our possession of the relationship we presume to isolate as the only thing in the world that interests us!

As we said towards the end this morning, our belonging to God is identified with total belonging, all-embracing belonging to one man. If God has become that Man, if that Man was assimilated, grasped and assimilated by God, then belonging to God coincides with belonging to Him. No human reason, even though it may view the hypothesis as absurd, can forbid the Infinite to commit a limitation.

Now we want to see what belonging to Christ in the whole of one's existence implies: "God is all in all," and so "Christ is all and in all." It is the event of a new humanity: in Christ is the event of a new humanity, in Christ we are born as a new man, different from the others. This event has a place where it is given and emerges: baptism, because baptism is the act with which Christ takes a life, elects and chooses a life. In Christ we are born as a new man, different from others, because we are baptized. Baptism, as the place where the Mystery dies inside human evil and rises by the divine power that it has within it, is the place where belonging to God acquires from God Himself a super-nature, a nature that is greater.

St Paul writes, "He chose us in him, before the foundation of the world, to be holy and without blemish before him. In love he destined us for adoption to himself through Jesus Christ, in accord with the favour of his will"[42] of the will of Christ, because it is Christ who chooses, God in Jesus of Nazareth. "The Spirit of God dwells in you. Whoever does not have the Spirit of Christ does not belong to him."[43]

So, it is in baptism that man is enabled to grow and become aware of himself, with an awareness that opens into an announcement of a relationship, an announcement in his soul of an exceptional, surpassing relationship, that "would exceed" his capacity. "Who could ever speak to us of Christ's love for man, overflowing with peace?"[44] But the new man is born, is conceived and is born differently from the natural man: second birth unexpectedly arrives after the first.

Now the interesting thing, the other interesting thing, is that every baptized person has an impressive bond with the others, which is a capacity to be united before every diversity: here the unity is given by the fact that every baptized person echoes the unity of God as mystery. So this is a mystery, it is a mysterious event.

If God has become one of us in order to enable us to live well, in other words to live faith in Christ, the condition for this is welcoming Christ and living with Him, sharing intimately in His life and therefore in His cross and resurrection (and the path for sharing intimately in His life is first of all the Church's liturgy). This makes man able to fulfil himself in the depth of a communion (so Gaber will never find on that road, what he says at the end, "I would be sure to change my life if I could begin to tell us," We instead are "obliged," it's the very definition of our history). If God has become one of us in order to enable us to live well, in other words to live faith in Christ, the condition is welcoming Christ, acknowledging our belonging to Christ, and therefore living with Him, in other words sharing intimately in the events of his life (through memory and the Church's liturgy), so as to be able to look at the other as part of yourself, realized in the depth of communion: from the depths of our being we are ontologically united by the Mystery that is communicated in the supreme sacramental sign that is the Church.

"If he had come as God," says St Augustine, "he would not have been recognized. For if he had come as God, he would not have come for those who were incapable of seeing God. As God, it cannot be said that he came or he went since as God he is present everywhere, and he cannot be contained in any place. How then did he come? In his visible humanity."[45]

One of the ancient Fathers of the Church, St Irenaeus of Lyons, affirms, "The Word of God came to live among men and became Son of man, in order to accustom man to welcome God and to accustom

God to make his dwelling place in man, according to the will of the Mystery,"[46] of the Father.

And St Bernard says, "God came in the flesh to reveal Himself to men who are flesh, and so that his goodness be recognized, manifesting Himself in humanity. Since God manifested Himself in man, his goodness can no longer be hidden. What better proof could he have given than that of taking up my flesh? [...] Just as He made himself small in becoming flesh, thus He showed Himself great in goodness; and He is all the dearer to me because He has lowered Himself so much."[47]

There can be no belonging to God that is not belonging to Christ. The chosen people, those who were called, are all part of this belonging to Christ, the God made man, the God who arose in man's history just as an ordinary man, who was killed for the people and rose from the dead, to whom the Mystery communicated power, in other words, the Spirit, communicated Itself, communicated power over all things. This is why we say that the meaning of history is Christ, Jesus of Nazareth.

Belonging to Christ is something that no longer leaves the I closed up in itself, with worries and preoccupations like everyone else. That for which the I is made and for which it does everything is a Presence.

The man chosen by God, the baptized, can no longer stay closed in himself, or be worried and concerned as everyone else is. It is for a Presence – through which he is made, and by which he feels made, and is aware of being made: the presence of Christ in his Church – that he lives and does everything.

This is why St Paul writes to the first Church of Corinth, "For the love of Christ impels us, once we have come to the conviction that one died for all; therefore, all have died. He indeed died for all, so that those who live might no longer live for themselves but for him who for their sake died and was raised."[48] This is how the Christians treated each other in the beginning, in that first spreading of Christianity. In the letter to the Romans, chapter 14, St Paul says, "None of us lives for oneself, and no one dies for oneself. For if we live, we live for the Lord and if we die, we die for the Lord; so then, whether we live or die, we are the Lord's."[49] And in the letter to the Galatians, he goes into greater detail, "I live, no longer I, but Christ lives in me; insofar as I now live in the flesh, I live by faith in the Son of God who has loved me and given himself up for me."[50] There is no human imagination that could possibly have invented these things.

So, the new man does have a preoccupation like everyone else, but it is different and is ordered before the instruments needed for the work, the work being a lived belonging to Christ, the awareness of belonging to Christ lived out.

In this spirit, to die for Christ and to breast-feed a child is the same thing. "For we are his handiwork, created in Christ Jesus for the good works that God has prepared in advance, that we should live in them."[51]

In this possession by God, to whom man acknowledges that he belongs because everything comes to him from God, man discovers God as a historical factor. Everything then is lived by the elect as the dynamics of this belonging; so, in the Christian people, constituted as such by a ritual, everything becomes almost scenic evidence (there is nothing left aside, nothing that is of no use, no relationship that reduces the stature of the soul and the heart); everything becomes almost scenic evidence, in other words dramatic evidence, and drama always characterizes the Christian people. Everything is Christ's work, through the dialogue with Christ and with the mode of His presence, with those beside Him and those who are strangers: dialogue and response.

We have neither shame nor hesitation in saying that we are different: we have a way of seeing and conceiving action that is completely different from that of other men.

When on 30 May last, we identified life with begging, and man's supreme need as a lively awareness of belonging to Christ and to God, we spoke of prayer as the supreme expression of our freedom, because prayer is the acknowledgment of the Being of which all is made.[52] This gives everything a powerful capacity for positivity: everything, even death. To the desperate cry of the pastor Brand, in Ibsen's play of the same name (that we have quoted so often), "Answer me, O God above / In death's jaws: Can human will, / Summed, avail no fraction still / Of salvation?"[53] answers the humble positivity of St Therese of the Child Jesus who writes, "Whenever I am charitable, it is Jesus alone who is acting through me."[54] It is the phrase in which the I of St Therese of the Child Jesus acknowledges her value in affirming that all her good, all her capacity for good, like the whole of her life is of the Lord, incarnate, died, and risen for us. "Whenever I am charitable, it is Jesus alone who is acting through me."

2. The Aim of Belonging

What is this new creature generated for? Why has God intervened and why does He intervene in the world to bring about this new creature? In other words, let's consider the aim of belonging.

The first thing that we have seen today is that belonging to God must become belonging to Christ and that with this a new man, a new creature, enters the world (when I heard these things during my first years in the seminary: "new man," I didn't understand them, and even when I left the seminary I had not understood them; I was to understand later – time is precious as an instrument of God).

FOR THE GLORY OF THE FATHER

The new creature is generated so that the Father's mysterious plan, through Christ, with His unconditional self-giving to the Father may be completed. With His unconditional self-giving to the Mystery, Christ changes me, too, with all the huge human throng that, according to God's mysterious plan, are crowding up to enter into the river whose waters are the history of salvation, in which all that has been revealed by that Jew of Nazareth may flow into the sea of Christ: so that the mystery of the Father be fulfilled in me and thus in the world. This is why the Father created man, because He wanted to be acknowledged by nothingness, by what is nothing. This absolute gratuitousness – in which the action of the conscious being is placed, that is, the action of a creature that recognizes that only God is – has thus found a possible way to multiply this paradoxical encounter indefinitely.

The first word that can be said as the aim of the need to live the awareness of belonging is this: the glory of the Father, in which the relationship between Being and nothing, between God and the creature, becomes clear (always bearing in mind that the I is the self-awareness of the whole cosmos, of creation).

Mysteriously, the Mystery created, wanted a dialogue with nothingness, with this beggar. We are nothing. The Mystery created mysteriously, It wanted a dialogue with nothingness, for that inconceivable, and for us indefinable, unity between the will of God who asks man, "Who am I for you?" and man who replies, "You are everything," or "I don't recognize You, I don't know who You are. I am free." Only the first of these expressions is right, is true, is not a lie. This is why we said in St Peter's Square on 30 May that the true man is the beggar.

The Mystery created mysteriously, it wanted a dialogue with nothingness, with the beggar, for His glory, for the glory of God. There are things whose substance, importance, and greatness we can sense, but we cannot grasp how they happen. The "how" will be clarified by eternity, for the present it begins to be at least the title of a problem whose factors gradually become clear.

A NEW PEOPLE

This beggar, the baptized man, did not remain alone, but became *"quasi arena in litore maris"* (as sands of the seashore),[55] a people, an "ethnic reality *sui generis*," as Paul VI described it.[56] This people is created by some who express themselves, and expand, taking in many whom God gives them; a people, therefore, which is created and led by God, through certain people whom God allows to express themselves with expansive force.

This people, at its height, is the sacramental sign of the presence of Christ (sacramental sign means that the sign not only identifies itself with the space of the Mystery, but the contents of which it is a sign is brought about, actually happens). So, it has a sensible, visible, tangible aspect, analogous to that which God made in the Incarnation, by becoming flesh. If it is not an incarnate reality, then it is not the place where God acts as Christ. The humanity of Jesus of Nazareth, which was called to participate in the mystery of the divine nature, prolongs itself, so that the way that the Father has decided, in a sensible, visible, tangible reality – this people, which has an intelligent and affective appearance – may come about. It is the mystical Body of Christ, in other words, the tangible body of Christ in which the invisible divinity invests regions that the Father gives to the Son. This invasion generates men with a new mentality and a new fecundity.

"May that grace that made the Church the Body of Christ make all the members of the charity [i.e., of love, all the members of that place where God has shown his love for men] remain compact and persevere in the unity of the Body. May this be our prayer,"[57] said St Fulgentius of Ruspe.

We Christians have our origin in the Church, the locus today of Christ and of the free initiative of the Spirit of Christ who makes belonging to him lively, understood, and desired. The historical condition for this passage to happen (the historical, de facto condition) is the charism. The charism is an intervention of the Spirit of Christ in order to increase belonging to Christ in the world: it is a fact of the history in which we are born, in which the Spirit takes us by surprise, that history in which the Father has placed us. The plan of the originating Mystery, of the Father, has placed us on a given path, on a given road within the Church; it has immersed us in the fact of Christ, it has made us participate by making us His, in terms of our awareness and affection. The charism remains, thus, the charity that Christ has for us in making us His: His as awareness and affection, in other words, as mentality and as the way of dealing with and realising human affectivity.

So the novelty lies in understanding how Christ, the Spirit of Christ, aims at fulfilling in us a new mentality, a way of looking, but also of judging and of drawing consequences from that judgment, a method of cognition in the full sense of the word, that is different, new, and a way of affection, in the broadest sense of the word, that permits a clear and true awareness of our relationship with all things, but, above all, a new type of dynamics, of the vibration of the very nature of natural love.

We Christians have our origin in the Church, the locus today of Christ and of the free initiative of the Spirit of Christ who makes our belonging to Him lively, understood, and desired. This indicates a duty, an ultimate law of our conscience that reaches the whole circle of man's horizon.

FOR THE HUMAN GLORY OF CHRIST

The aim of all this, the aim for which the new man entered the world, is the human glory of Christ. Christ's invasion of reality is humanly unassailable, but in creating a physical situation like a body – in the individual, the group, the community – it becomes physically an object of persecution, precisely because of the truth and love that Christ arouses, in the cause of the power of truth, of the greatness and faithfulness of the love that Christ arouses.

What has already happened can still happen again, as Eliot says when he speaks of the need for Christians to build altars, altars that the enemies will destroy; after this destruction a new era of building will follow. This alternation will go on as long as God wants it.[58]

So, for the Christian – and this is important as a criterion for our way of thinking and as the true quality of love – it is impossible to have a taste for hegemony, for winning power, because this is of God, it is God who indicates it.

In every moment of the development of this body, persecution is possible, but so is the ascent of humanity, which thus becomes filled with the perception of Christ's presence, of the miracle of a moral change and of an aesthetic commitment. Along with the truth acknowledged by our intelligence, this humanity can give birth to a new society, that can reach such a level as to normally seem incomprehensible to man and his measure. It is a society that can appear as sacramental in history from many points of view, like that of the Middle Ages, in certain periods of the Middle Ages.

The ultimate meaning of the cosmos (in which this human history is contained), that happens along the whole course of the life of this people – that goes from John and Andrew up to the Son of Man who will return on the last day – is Jesus of Nazareth, into whose hands the Father has given everything.[59] It is the Father who chooses the people and acknowledges his holiness in those who acknowledge the fulfilment of the Covenant, in those who He sees living their belonging to Him intensely (like, for example, Anna and Simeon, among the remnant of Israel, Mary and Joseph). Since, however, the Father has given everything into the Son's hands, the origin of the vocation of the individual, the beginning of the people of the Church and the fulfilment of this is a man, Jesus of Nazareth, the presence of Being, the Mystery, God to me. It is a reality that began two thousand years ago. So, the life of a Christian is a memory, in terms of dynamics, and is certitude, in other words, hope in the promises that Jesus introduces, that they be fulfilled in every man He has called. I always think of this when, in the *Angelus*, we say that beautiful prayer in which we ask God that we, who by the message of an angel have come to know of his Incarnation, may be brought through His death and resurrection to share in the glory of Christ. The glory of all our actions, in other words the formation of the principle for which we live, of the Presence to which we are committed, is a man, Jesus of Nazareth, called Christ for this reason, the Messiah the Jews were waiting for: and instead, in order to save the people, they killed him.

This new I knows in a new way and it becomes fond, positively, of all beings, within a limit (the limit established by creation, in other words according to their original nature), in everything it does for the sake of God's plan, that is to say, Christ's plan.

A Christian therefore has to love Christ. For a Christian who is conscious, who accepts all the inevitable circumstances of his life as the expression of his belonging to the Mystery, to God, the expression of his awareness of this belonging, everything must lead back to and spring from loving Christ. So, love for Christ is the dynamics of all relationships with things, with every person, it is the ultimate criterion and the measure of everything, the aim of every action. The consequence of love for Christ is facing up to everything according to Christ's own mentality, taking on Christ's mentality.

There are certain problems, briefly listed here, that constitute the fundamental factors of social life: work, the problem of affectivity (the satisfaction of the affective problem), justice. The three terms in which we have tried to identify all the fervour, the capacity for action, the whole commitment of human freedom – work, affection or the affective problem, justice – are themes we have already in some way touched upon, of which we already know some developments; but I hope they will be deepened in the life of our communities.

THE PASSAGE TO THE ULTIMATE MEANING: FAITH, HOPE, AND CHARITY

One last observation. We have said that we need to love Christ in all the inevitable circumstances of our life, according to His mode of dynamics and His mode of affectivity. Thus, is conceived the final step of our awareness of belonging to the meaning of being, of the cosmos and of all history: it is the last Judgment. No-one knows the day of this Judgment, only the Father, the Mystery as origin knows it. It is the Father who establishes his mysterious plan, in which the history of the Christian people knows good times and bad, analogously to the flow of history of the Jewish people. This is, or should be, a very evident principle in the life of a Christian.

The most evident difference in the Christian man in terms of his mentality (that is to say, as intelligence and affection, because a characteristic of the Christian way of thinking, or mentality, is that of indicating a deep, original link between knowing and loving; so we say, normally, that a love that is shared – and therefore a friendship – can arise only from a judgment: love that does not arise from a judgment is not human), the most evident difference in the Christian man's mentality, that is to say, in intelligence and love, in comparison to someone who does not belong to Christ is the fact that he lives the conditions of existence and of history starting from a positive certainty about everything. It is impossible to sustain this position outside the Christian event.

Let's think for example of parents faced with the loss of a child, or a Christian community initially enthusiastic which then loses its form, like some of the early communities described in the Apocalypse of St John: "I know your works. I know that you are neither cold nor hot. I wish you were either cold or hot! So, because you are lukewarm, neither hot nor cold, I will spit you out of my mouth. For you say, 'I am rich and affluent, and have no need of anything,' and yet do not realize that you are wretched, pitiable, poor, blind, and naked."[60]

Think of our families, of the individual, when something serious happens in life; he had always thought that for a believer life could not have such tough contradictions, but now, in the hour of a trial, he is brought to affirm his hope. Accepting the trials that God sends intelligently, and understanding that the Lord sends them so that the affection we have for Him may grow, is always an increase in holiness, it is an increase in the awareness of one's belonging.

If this capacity for hope fails, then certain experiences of the Church try to save themselves a place in the world, assuming their own criteria as a source of dignity and respect (the opposite of all this lies in the fact that a Christian man tries to affirm his hope in the world). This would be the symptom of a belonging to Christ that is fading away, and for such a belonging Christ's dramatic question regarding the day and the hour that not even the Son knows resounds: "But when the Son of Man comes, will he find faith on earth?"[61]

This is the principal test of the faith! Faith in Christ is acknowledging Christ present, the foundation of our hope: in every circumstance, even before death. Thus, the final step to the meaning of the existence of the cosmos and of the whole of history, that is the last Judgment is conceived: the final passage to meaning, in other words, the extreme answer to the whole problem of belonging. And the reaching of this level, the acknowledgment of the ultimate aim of belonging, is a prize, a prize that verifies and confirms, confirms and verifies the great value of belonging as a word that matures in our heart.

Being Christian is belonging to Christ, to how the person of Christ showed Himself to man. The figure of Christ expresses itself, spreads within the history of a people. Our belonging to Christ coincides, therefore, with our belonging to the people of Christ, to the Church of God. And our way of living the Church of God is the charism.

St Paul said to the first Christians of Salonica:

God did not destine us for wrath but to gain salvation through
our Lord Jesus Christ, who died for us, so that whether we
are awake or asleep we may live together with him. Therefore,
encourage one another and build one another up, as indeed you
do. [...] Rejoice always. Pray without ceasing. In all circumstances give thanks, for this is the will of God for you in Christ
Jesus. Do not quench the Spirit. do not despise prophetic utter-
ances. Test everything; retain what is good.[62]

This is the discovery of Christian culture. In the small group at the
start of GS [*Gioventù Studentesca* – Student Youth], the definition of
culture we immediately gave was this text of St Paul, "Do not despise
prophecies; examine everything and keep what is of value." But why
should we compare everything with this encounter in such a way that
the value be a word applicable to it? This is the perennial discovery
that is born from belonging to Christ: an affection for all things.

That positivity I mentioned before is an affection for all things,
in other words a sharing in the *caritas*, in the gratuitousness with
which God has looked at everything and made everything and does
everything for his creature.

Another prayer of the Church for Saturday in the fifth week of
Lent says, "O God, kind and faithful, who create the existence
of man and renew it [with the call of Abraham which develops and
develops in the history of the Jewish people, God was waiting for the
moment of his total answer to faithfulness that was in his people,
the age in which Christ came: God became man, Christ came, this
is the renewal of man, the renewing of man's existence], look with
favour on the people you have chosen and call new generations
untiringly to your covenant so that, according to your promise, they
may rejoice to receive as a gift that dignity of the children of God
that exceeds, beyond all hope, the very capacity of their nature."[63]

This prayer of the Church is really a synthesis of what the Christian
must have as the contents of his self-awareness and as guidelines
for the deepening of his awareness of what has happened, and as
affective attachment to Christ. Because if man's problem is love for
the Father, love for the Mystery, then the Christian man's problem
becomes love for Christ. But love for Christ is the way in which
the Mystery has wished to educate mankind: through what we have

touched, through what we touch, because Jesus, love for Jesus, is a love that is conscious, a great affection for His body, and love for His body, affection for His body is the life of our communities.

ASSEMBLY AND SYNTHESIS

GIANCARLO CESANA: Yesterday evening we carried out our traditional work of revision in the hotels; this year these assemblies really tried to gather the discussion into one question. An initial note: almost all the questions that arrived regard the first lesson; this means that the second has to be read and attentively taken up again, given its centrality and synthetic quality. The first question is this: why was the term "belonging" given preference this year, after last year's insistence on the term "knowledge"?

LUIGI GIUSSANI: We insisted on the term "belonging" because the content of knowledge is first of all cultivated and brought to expression, that is to say communicated, by a criterion, that is also called mentality, proper to that to which we belong. Whether or not we are aware of it, the way in which we feel, see, and judge comes from what we belong to. This is why we are not being Christians, we cannot claim to be Christians, if, with the help of God, we do not try to look at things, all things – in our own life, but also in the life of the world, like the awful events of these days – and, praying to God, we do not become able to answer to them with a criterion that we have received from the Church to which we belong.

STEFANO ALBERTO (FR PINO): This is a question that came up many times, "Can you explain better the relationship between belonging and freedom?" Because according to the normal way of thinking – our friends in one hotel wrote – belonging, being-of, is considered as a denial of freedom. Whereas you spoke of freedom as an essential factor and the first consequence of belonging. And then, "Why is there a rebellion at the idea of the I as belonging?"

GIUSSANI: If belonging is depending, being made, the awareness of still being made, continuously made by the Creator, by God, by the Mystery of God, then what have we received from the Mystery of God? Everything! And therefore, what we can call freedom, too. Thus, belonging is the source of freedom. This can be lived out to a greater or lesser extent, but the extent depends not only on freedom, but also on another factor, which is the will of the Mystery, the mysterious will of God. Anyway, I think it is exhaustive to say that, if belonging indicates the factor that has given us and still gives us being, the energy that constitutes in us an attitude of freedom comes from belonging. For freedom does not create itself.

CESANA: But if that's the case, why do we rebel against it so much?

GIUSSANI: We rebel first of all because we don't know the terms of the question, people don't know what freedom is, they have never reflected on it. However, the word is used by everyone, because it is a word that arises from our experience (all the things that interest man have to be grasped from the experience he has). And everyone uses the word according to the currents of thought, or of interests, or of power. But sifting through the interpretation and going down to the essentials, it seems to me that, as we said two years ago, freedom is acknowledging Him who gives us being, Him who makes us; Him who creates us, and all that sincerely and actively collaborates, that is taken by God as an instrument for realizing His ideas for our life, His images of our existence. For the sake of completion, this compels us to say that freedom is acknowledging that God is all in all, almost as if God made the world and creation in order to challenge nothingness (these are mere figures of speech, but I can't find better ones to explain what freedom is and what creation is), almost as if God wanted His creature to be a reality that should acknowledge that He is all, as the echo of a glory that is within the Mystery.

The final aspect of the question asked is about why there is this rebellion. It is almost ridiculous to ask this question, because we do not touch and cannot exhaust the Mystery, the relationship between Mystery and creature. In the end, in my opinion, we are unable to say why someone refuses the greatest evidence there is. The question becomes more urgent and annoying because when we think of the devil (*daimon*), the rebel angel, who not without reason can be defined as one who doesn't acknowledge to have been made by Another ("No, I don't acknowledge You, You are not the one who gave me being."), it seems to us a denial, a lie that seems a denial. There is an aspect of this situation that remains shrouded in mystery. Freedom cannot be defined in other terms and rebellion cannot be explained; it can be explained only as a gloomy silence to oneself, before the last door which is that of feeling that we are created, feeling made; "I don't acknowledge You." But nothing can eliminate what comes before, that God is all in all; Being is all in all beings.

CESANA: How can the temptation to hegemony be avoided in the historical responsibility that Christians have?

GIUSSANI: Hegemony as the motive for one's commitment is avoided when one is not committed with the thirst for success that comes from self-esteem, or from selfishness, or from self-interest (selfishness or self-interest); in this case the opposition between hegemony and historical responsibility is resolved. Having said this about hegemony, that is a *hỳbris* that emerges from the web of violence that (unfortunately) dominates our days, let's take a look at the Christian's historical responsibility. We need to use another name in order to speak of it, not a hegemonic will for personal success, out of personal pride, as a prize or a collection of things that one wants. The Christian's historic responsibility is something else: given by the fact that love for Christ, in which we share in the Church, love for Christ who personally invades our soul, leads us to a commitment that has another name and a different nature. It is taking an interest in the life of others, of all men, using all the ways and means that God puts at man's disposal, and that are just – just! But the charity that drives us is not, cannot be called tendency to hegemony. The Christian must try to fight for his faith or for freedom and justice towards others, even by trying to win posts of power, but if he doesn't get there, it was not his aim, success is not his ultimate duty, because the circumstances in which God leaves him and sets him to work, may not allow him this. Even Jesus Himself, who came to bring peace to the world, was killed!

FR PINO: Here is a more precise question, that refers to a passage in the first lesson: "What do you mean when you say that even justice must be judged by the law of belonging?"

GIUSSANI: Justice is not something hanging in the air, a star, it does not act in the air without an active subject. So, a man who judges another man must be able to do so with his conscience following a law of God, because that man belongs to God as you or I do. But, if he has this awareness, he cannot judge a man in order to gain political advantage, for example, or in order to further his career as a magistrate. So, I think that it is very hard, very difficult to comply with, to obey the law of God in many things, for me as a priest just as for a judge (although I don't judge in the courts, before God I can do it: after all, confession is a kind of tribunal, isn't it?). There is one particular fact that comes to the surface and that helps us understand that there is something murky underneath: it is the absence of love for the person. I quoted Nietzsche's phrase in this sense: "From the eyes of your judges gazes always the executioner and his cold steel."[64] Because apart from everything else, it is always – always – against the ultimate true interests of society, if a judge, who represents society in that sector, heads off with an apparently exasperated, exaggerated reading of the code of law, without keeping in mind the things we said: his own dependence on God.

CESANA: On the other hand, we can also say that since we always depend, either on God or on Mammon, as was said earlier, especially if one does not realize this, he judges according to the power that predominates.

GIUSSANI: Of course! However, the predominant power succeeds – through all the means it has, more and more invasive of the personality, psychologically more and more able to introduce a dimension that is common to everyone, in many things – if we don't already belong to something, not provisionally, but as a judgment about ourselves, about what we are and what we are doing in the world, as you heard yesterday in the words of the first apostles, St John and St Paul, "None of us lives for oneself, and no one dies for oneself. For if we live, we live for the Lord, and if we die, we die for the Lord."[65]

CESANA: The question I am about to read describes a situation that is quite widespread, and is expressed in elementary but clear terms: "There is an equation that makes me tremble. The God of Abraham who reveals Himself in Christ, who continues in the Church and has reached us with your charism, is incarnate in persons, persons who have positions of responsibility in my community, to whom I am to obey: this is a problem for me. What does it mean to belong through obeying these persons?"

GIUSSANI: "Obedience" is a word that should come to the surface a lot in the reflection that we have introduced this year. Because if man is born of Another – if I am made by Another – evidently, he must obey this Other. If it is set before That which it derives from, obedience is the virtue that ensures the development of what is given it. What happens instead is that obedience is forcefully and bitterly objected to, firstly as a temptation of our consciousness, in an age like ours in which the data and the events of our consciousness, both natural and revealed by God, by Jesus, are absolutely not observed, that is to say, not understood and therefore set aside, because they appear to be a denial of our freedom, of a freedom or of an enjoyment, and seem contrary to life. But it is precisely to That on which we depend, to That which made us, it is precisely to Him that we owe obedience. Because nothing of you is yours, originally yours, everything is given to you. And it was given to you not without intelligence and love. The Father, who is in heaven, has a plan for you; what you are given in order to live and exist is marked by "signs" in its development – what it consists of and how it must be used – and these are the laws, the moral laws (moral law is not invented by man, but is made by a man who is aware of his origin). At the origin the phenomena of development of the capacities that man must have, are indicated. So, obedience as a virtue is proper to the Christian. For Christ made Himself obedient unto death, death on a cross. Everything in our life seems to be made, seems to speak against this word. On the other hand, the criterion with which we live things, what we desire, how we try to get what we desire, what is useful for us, what we see as beautiful, the criterion (we have seen it during these days) ultimately comes from Another. Obedience is doing things according to Another's criterion. If man is made by God, then his whole life depends on God. That is why we began the Spiritual Exercises, three years ago, by saying, "God is all in all." But, according to the modern way of thinking, the operator, in other words man, man who works, who is molded, made by God, made of God present in him from the origin, has as it were abandoned his origin: the origin is taken for granted and so clouds over in time, until it vanishes. In its place, through our schoolmates, these days from kindergarten right through to university, more and more, and with ever greater arrogance, the world, says Christ, offers us its judgments, its invitations, its advice, and its attractions. And we grow up, we seem to grow up precisely because, having forgotten our origin, we go against a duty, against our duty. Not obeying anyone, or rather, not obeying our own father and mother, not obeying the past, the proposals that due to the past we feel like following, putting into practice, not obeying has become something classic for man. The break with the past is the genius of the ministers of education of our governments.

CESANA: On the other hand, someone who obeys is looking for the charism, in other words, he is looking for the origin, and the one who calls attention to this is not calling attention to himself, but to the charism, to what the Church has recognized.

GIUSSANI: Thank you for that observation, because you have touched on a very interesting corollary regarding the problem of obedience to the Church and to the movement, which seems often not to correspond or be convincing. But what you hear from us is convincing in proportion with your simplicity and sincerity. Otherwise, God must have made a mistake in becoming man! Because if He had not become a man there would not have been all these consequences. But, as St Gregory Nazianzen said, "If I weren't yours, my Christ, I would feel a finished creature,"[66] I would not be a man, because being man was given by You. God wanted to come and speak among men without hope, who were scattered and bewildered by confusion; God became a man, a man among us: as two thousand years ago, now He is among us. And here is the point of origin, Christ could have said and thought as man, "Am I here forever, has the Father given the whole world into my hands and am I here to save it? But if I accept to die, if I accept to be crucified, what will happen next?" So, it was then, at that point that He imagined how to be present, according to His ideal, the ideal that the Father, the Mystery of God had inoculated into that human heart, His human heart: He thought up this great thing that is the Church; the Church that begins to show itself where two or three are gathered in His name (and this is the principle of our fraternity, of the Fraternity). But the head of your community may be someone mediocre, unexceptional. And yet we've been accustomed to not having this objection by God and by the popes we have known, who have been really great, truly men of faith and of an intelligent faith. As with the Church, all the more so with the movements in the Church, all that participates in the Church:

dioceses, parishes, movements, all three proclaim clearly that the word of God and the grace of God are communicated through hands that tremble, like when you are seventy years old, and so your hand trembles: and people receive the host from a hand that trembles as they would receive it when the hand was steady! But the Church is valid, because Christ made it and therefore Christ cannot abandon it; because the Spirit descended on the apostles and Our Lady, in the beginning, and gave itself to the whole of mankind: Christ remains here for everyone, until the end of time.

So, in the communities some have roles; what is necessary is that what they say be perfectly equal to what every Christian, as a duty of his role, or simply of charity, of relationships must respect and love with perfection. Obedience is the hardest thing for knights, for friars, and for lay people in the movements.

* * *

I want to leave you a wish. After all you have heard it might not be understood, but I do it all the same because there's nothing better I can say.

I wish that in your life, having encountered this great thing, which is a grace of God, as now we hear said naturally and spontaneously in every place where there is one of us ... through the grace of this encounter that we have been given, there is a potential in you, a potential in you that the Spirit has put there, implicitly or more explicitly, according to each one's own history, a capacity that the Spirit has put into you for witnessing to Christ, who is the only thing the world is waiting for, because where Christ is, relationships are peaceful, united and peaceful, including those between married couples (unity and peace must be the binomial of the family; but this is true for everyone). In any case, whatever the form of your vocation, my wish is that in this great thing, through this great thing that the Lord has given you, if it becomes more and more personal, that is to say more obedient (because personalization, too, is obedience lived out intelligently), you may meet a father, you may have the experience of a father. Because the first belonging, physiologically and sociologically speaking, and even to your own eyes, is to your parents. God is given to us through our father and mother.

May each one of you discover the greatness of this role, which is not a role; it is the condition in which man looks at and sees God, and in which God entrusts to man what he most wants; father and therefore mother, because it's the same thing, spiritually they are not two different things; it is only materially that things change, when one has his own limitation and the other a different one. So, this is why I wanted to come here to greet you. May you live the experience of a father; father and mother; this is my wish for all the leaders, for all those responsible for your communities, but for each one of you, too, because each one has to be father to the friends he has around him, has to be mother of the people around about; not giving himself airs, but with real charity. For no-one can be as fortunate and glad as a man and a woman who feel themselves made fathers and mothers by the Lord. Fathers and mothers of all those they meet. Do you remember – as the second book of the School of Community describes it – when Jesus was walking through the fields with his apostles, near the town of Naim, and saw a woman weeping as she followed her dead son to his burial? He went up to her; He didn't say, "I'm going to raise your son." He said, "Woman, don't weep," with a tenderness, affirming an unmistakable tenderness and love for the human person! And then He gave her back her son alive.[67] But this isn't the point, because even other people can work miracles, but this charity, this love for man that is proper to Christ is quite beyond compare! Let's go.

Speeches and Greetings

2000–2004

Beginning in 2000, Fr Giussani no longer preached the Spiritual Exercises of the Fraternity of Communion and Liberation. Even the pre-recorded video format became too burdensome, due to his worsening health, and the sustained speech required to give a lesson or meditation became impossible for him. This entailed an enormous sacrifice for him, who had identified some of the principal causes of faith's lack of influence on the life of modern man in the absence of reasons when proposing the Christian message and in the incapacity to communicate how faith responded to the concrete, human questions of life.

Still, as was his custom, he did not give up and continued to express, albeit in a different way, what he was discovering within life's circumstances: the fruit of his self-awareness; the reflections inspired in him by literature, music, or current events; and his reactions and judgments regarding communal life, which were always very perceptive. They took the form of speeches at conferences, the reading of which was entrusted to his collaborators, interviews and articles in national newspapers, messages to CL communities on particular occasions or at the time of large gatherings, letters to the Fraternity – notably in 2002 and 2004 – and television programs. After an attack on Italian soldiers at Nassiriya and after their funeral in Rome, which unified the country in mourning, the director of the Channel 2 News for the Italian national television network asked Fr Giussani to write the text for the opening page of the 8:30 evening news. The reflection that was broadcast commented on Carducci's *Ancient Lament*, Canto 33 of Dante's *Paradiso*, and the judgment given on air by Brigadier Coletta's wife, and called for a renewal of the people, an education of people's hearts. "If there were an education of the people, everyone would live better."[1] The news channel used another of his meditations for their program on Christmas Eve in 2004. It would be Giussani's last public interview, in which he said, among other things, "Christmas, the Nativity, is Christ's love for man. […] The new Being is coming into the world."[2] One month earlier, he had chosen the following words from Cesare Pavese for the text of the CL Christmas poster: "The only joy in the world is to begin. It is good to be alive because living is beginning, always, every moment."[3] In his prayer intention for the masses marking the 23rd anniversary of the pontifical recognition of the Fraternity, Fr Giussani invited everyone to "risk" living as Christ did and defined the Fraternity as "the place where we immediately understand what our own origin is."[4]

The Exercises continued to develop a defined logic of a discourse centred on the nature of the I and the personalization of the faith, with eloquent titles: *What Is Man and How Does He Come to Know It* (2000); *Abraham: The Birth of the "I"* (2001); *The Life I Now Live in the Flesh I Live by Faith in the Son of God* (2002); *Event of Freedom* (2003); and *The Destiny of Man* (2004).

Fr Giussani remotely participated in the meetings from his own residence, addressing the participants gathered in Rome or connected by video at the end of the weekend with his own greetings, with the exception of the 2003 Exercises.

His words were for the most part unscripted, expressing his reaction at what he had just heard, and pregnant with thought, emotion, and love for all those who were listening to him in the great hall of the Rimini Fiera by phone, or seeing him on the screen through videoconference. His memorable words ("Woman, do not weep"; the "*Veni Sancte Spiritus*"; the "positivity of our life") were repeated over and over again by his friends, and entered their individual consciousness, leaving an indelible mark. They, like so many other words he spoke, made Fr Giussani a familiar presence in each person's life, both at the time and still today.

After sharing the responsibilities of leading previous editions, giving a lesson, or helping in the final assembly, Fr Julián Carrón first preached the entire Fraternity Exercises in 2004. In his intrusion by video conference, Fr Giussani externalized his enthusiasm and confident endorsement for all he had heard.

Hope Does Not Disappoint was the title of the 2005 Exercises, which took place after Fr Luigi Giussani passed away on 22 February of the same year.

———————

"WHAT IS MAN AND HOW DOES HE COME TO KNOW IT?"

(Giussani's Final Speech at the Spiritual Exercises of the Fraternity of Communion and Liberation, Rimini, 19–21 May 2000)

I am speaking to you ... it is the whole day, the whole of yesterday, and the day before, it is the whole of life that we have been talking, because what is contained in our first songs is really true, right from the contents of our first songs.

1) "I am not worthy of what You do for me, You who love someone like me so much."[5] It's a very bitter fact that God has made us grow in a charity and in a lively awareness of what man's life is, of what that movement is, of all the Church is, of what man's end is, what his destiny is – his destiny coincides with his end – and we are so unworthy.

"I am not worthy of what You do for me." Think how, with every day that passes, I increase in myself the wonder at what God does! And God makes today because He has made yesterday! This is why it is a new reality in the world, which has entered the world; it is a new unity that has entered the world of the Church – and so we can also, or rather we must also add that a new reality within the Church increases, makes blossom more lovingly and more brilliantly what the Church is.

You see, "I am not worthy of what You do for me, I who have nothing to give to You." However, I tell You, "If You want, take me."

2) I was thinking over again these days about all the huge amount of life and thought there has been among us. Because it's very significant that the first song that happened among us (I say "happened" because that's how it was) should already express the whole dimension of the question – in other words the reason – that moves us; and on the other hand, has already given the answer.

Try to think of the hymn of our movement, of those words written by Maretta Campi, with the music of Adriana Mascagni: "If our voice is a voice that no longer has a reason, then it's the poor voice of a man who doesn't exist." But "it must cry out and implore that the breath of life may not end." The jolt that we spoke about, that they spoke about so well this morning, the great jolt of the desire for life, with emotion, with commitment, with the emotion of feeling, with the commitment of freedom, could also be felt as a need to bring about.

"The poor voice of a man who doesn't exist": if this voice were not to have a reason, it would be deceitful and empty. Therefore, if it must cry out and implore that the breath of life may not end, it must also "sing because there is life." This is the immense reason, that cannot be compared with any other word. "The whole of life asks for eternity." When we get up in the morning for a frenetic day, a tiresome day, or for a day free from particular engagements, "it must sing because there is life; the whole of life asks for eternity."

The whole of life asks for eternity. Try to think of forty years in which the whole of life has asked for eternity! "It cannot die, it cannot end, this voice of ours that asks love for life." This is why "it is not the poor voice of a man who doesn't exist: our voice sings with a reason."[6]

As I was thinking these days of who composed this song, with its words and its music – they were two friends, fifteen or sixteen years old – I was asking myself, who these days can find such a synthetic and lively expression, capable of petition, that anyone can recognize as serious and sincere?

3) When Judas stopped staying with Jesus and went out to betray him, the Gospel says, *"Erat autem nox"*[7]: it was night.

To forget, or to let go what we have been told, what we are told, would be to have our whole life fall into that darkness into which the life of the great majority of men seems destined to fall.

We go ahead in life through a certitude that burns away all that threatens us and all the fears for the strength we might lack.

Hope for us is a certainty, a certainty for the future. For someone who walks without certainty about where he has to get to, it would be like the tragedy of a poor man.

We let darkness overcome us too often, above all more than the desire for truth there is the delusion of a doubt.

"If a man has everything but has no forgiveness, tell me how he can hope."[8] This verse from a song by our Claudio Chieffo is perhaps the most human and overpowering observation that there is.

"If a man has everything but has no forgiveness, how can he hope"; if he does not recognize forgiveness which is the most dramatic and most convincing aspect of the relationship that the Mystery has with us, in such a way that he does not accept forgiveness as the supreme form of the relationship between himself and other men (the Lord's

Prayer says: "forgive us our trespasses as we forgive those who trespass against us"). The man for whom what prevails is the sense of his own nothingness, the feeling of his discouragement, dominates, though, and he allows himself to be dominated, he becomes a slave of what the world says. And the world, sooner or later, manages to deny the certainty of human happiness.

Erat autem nox: it was night. The darkness into which the source of our hope and its power fall, is helped along by us, since that hope is not an answer that appears immediately living and realized. So, we are like the awareness of a man when he is at the level of imposture. Thus, all the advantage of our friendship, of our Fraternity, all the advantage of the Church in history is obscured, too.

All the negativity prevails when man is Judas, when he cannot avoid this identification with Judas, with the betrayer; but instead of crying out he should implore that the destiny of life may not end.

Anyway, there would have been nothing in the world that could have really helped us. But as we "need someone to free us from evil,"[9] God has made Himself; the Mystery has made Himself tangibly present, flesh of our flesh.

To look at Jesus in the womb of His mother is the most liberating, the greatest thing we can imagine. Let's help each other to walk more and more in the light of this, so that the draining of our energy not obscure the truth of the light.

"ABRAHAM: THE BIRTH OF THE I"

(Giussani's Final Speech at the Spiritual Exercises of the Fraternity of Communion and Liberation, Rimini, 18–20 May 2001)

I was able to follow your progress in the manner the Lord has permitted me, more limited and laborious than before. But everything is a progress of God in our life. In any case, this is the only formula for making our heart morally, also morally ready, and ever able to suffer, for the way God made us.

But, so as not to keep you there too long, I say today that there is only one thing that we cannot miss (let's not drop it as a possibility): we must pray in the literal sense of the term, in other words, we must beseech Him to Whom we belong, that He may not have called us in vain.

Every day we are called, every hour we are called, every minute, every instant we are called. For what qualifies the I, what defines the I in the face of all the other human attitudes, what qualifies the I is precisely the consciousness that it is relationship with the Infinite: a woman is sewing, she is sewing or cooking in the kitchen, and she is relationship with the Infinite. What characterizes man is this paradoxical dimension between the little that he is, the very little that he is, the fuse that he is, between a littleness that he is and the constitutive relationship, a constitutive relationship which is the relationship with God.

But now I do not want to take up again things that we have already taken up together. I want simply to say: let us pray, let us pray, because this is something we can do even while we are doing any other task. It is an intention, it opens us to an intention, just as on a rainy day the sun breaks through the clouds, pierces the clouds and throws light, it makes us throw light on everything we are and do.

I have applied in recent times, I have discovered in recent times, with all my heart, deeply moved, the jaculatory formula, so to speak, the most complete formula that can be conceived from the Christian point of view: "Come, Holy Spirit. Come through Our Lady." *Veni Sancte Spiritus. Veni per Mariam.* Repeat this formula every day, at all hours, when the Lord chooses you to make Himself heard: it is a moment in which everything is reconnected and reconquered, everything is made a unique and beautiful thing.

Veni Sancte Spiritus, because *Spiritus est Dominus, Spiritus est Deus* (God is Spirit, the Spirit is God). The Spirit is God, to Whom we belong. Because the Spirit is consciousness of self; and if this is applied properly in us it makes us understand: man understands that he belongs, that he is belonging to Another. It is belonging to a Presence, to a Presence, here too, that is mysterious (mysterious because it is not ours, this Presence, in a certain sense it is not; because if it comes from another source, it is not from our source).

"Come, Holy Spirit" into my every action, "Come, Holy Spirit" into my every moment.

Veni per Mariam, and this is precisely ... Our Lady is precisely the most powerfully human and persuasive touch that God has made towards His acting on man.

Veni per Mariam. Think of the evolution of this woman and Her way of lasting even in history! But obviously the foundation of Her belonging is from God, is in God. Yet, on the other hand,

Mary is the totality of man, the totality of man who is exalted to the point of making Her become, of rendering Her the necessary instrument for relationship with God (necessary, not in the immediate sense of the term, but in the ultimate sense of the term). *Per Mariam*, because She did not make a single mistake, God did not allow Her to be the object of attack by the demon opposed to the truth. Virgin pure and beautiful: beauty is the sign, and She is as it were a sacramental sign of the beauty of which God made the world.

So then, happy to have left you a reminder of this jaculatory, this insurgent, always insurgent glory of our Christian life, may the *Veni Sancte Spiritus. Veni per Mariam*; Mariam be a support, may it reveal itself to be a psychologically clear support, because it is profoundly permeated with origin, with roots.

My wish for you is that this jaculatory, that this surge of sincerity and simplicity, may daily find in your hearts space to be recalled and human reality to be changed in accordance with that ultimate order for which we were made. And destiny is this, and this is what we are missing so many times, but that never ceases for an instant: God cannot cease for even an instant being the wellspring of our happiness, of our fruitfulness.

"THE LIFE I NOW LIVE IN THE FLESH, I LIVE BY FAITH IN THE SON OF GOD"

(Giussani's Final Speech Final Speech at the Spiritual Exercises of the Fraternity of Communion and Liberation, Rimini, 3–5 May 2002)

That evening Jesus was interrupted, stopped on His journey to the village towards which He was heading, to which He had headed out, because loud weeping was heard from a woman, with a cry of pain that shook the hearts of all those present, but that shook, has shaken Christ's heart first of all.[10]

"Woman, do not weep!"[11] He had never seen her, never met her before.

"Woman, do not weep!" What support could she have, that woman as she listened to the words that Jesus said to her?

"Woman, do not weep!" When we return home, when we go on the bus, when we climb aboard the train, when we see the cars lined up in the streets, when we think about all the jumble of things that are involved in the lives of millions and millions of people, hundreds of millions of people ... . How decisive is the look that a child or a "great" adult would have turned on this Man who was coming along at the head of a small group of friends and had never seen that woman, but halted when the sound, the reverberation of her weeping reached Him! "Woman, do not weep!" – as though no one knew her, no one could recognize her more intensely, more totally, more decisively than He!

"Woman, do not weep!" When we see – as I said to you before – all the movement in the world, in whose river, in whose streams all men present themselves to life and make life present to them, the unknown of the end is nothing but the unknown of how this newness has been reached, this newness that makes us come upon a Man, makes us encounter a Man never seen before who, faced with the pain of this woman He sees for the first time, says to her: "Woman, do not weep!"; "Woman, do not weep!"

"Woman, do not weep!" This is the heart with which we are placed before the gaze and the sadness, before the pain of all the people with whom we come into contact, in the street, along our way, in our travels.

"Woman, do not weep!" What an unimaginable thing it is that God – God, He who is making the whole world at this moment – seeing and listening to man, could say: "Man, do not weep!"; "You, do not weep!"; "Do not weep, because I did not make you for death, but for life! I put you in the world and placed you in a great company of people!"

Man, woman, boy, girl, you, all of you, do not weep! Do not weep! There is a gaze and a heart that penetrates to your very marrow and loves you all the way to your destiny, a gaze and a heart that no one can deflect from His course, no one can render incapable of saying what He thinks and what He feels, no one can render powerless!

"*Gloria Dei vivens homo.*"[12] The glory of God, the greatness of Him who makes the stars in the sky, who puts into the sea, drop by drop, all the blue that defines it, is man who lives.

There is nothing that can suspend that immediate rush of love, of attachment, of esteem, of hope. Because He became hope for each one who saw Him, who heard Him: "Woman, do not weep!"; who heard Jesus say this: "Woman, do not weep!"

There is nothing that can block the certainty of a destiny that is mysterious and good!

We are together, saying to each other: "You, I have never seen you, I don't know who you are: do not weep!" Because weeping is your destiny, it seems to be your unavoidable destiny: "Man, do not weep!"

"*Gloria Dei vivens homo.*" The glory of God – the glory for whom He holds up the world, the universe – is man who lives, every man who lives: the man who lives, the woman who weeps, the woman who smiles, the child, the woman who dies a mother.

"*Gloria Dei vivens homo.*" We want this and nothing but this, that the glory of God be manifested to all the world and touch all the spheres of earth: the leaves, all the leaves of the flowers and all the hearts of men.

We have never seen each other, but this is what we see among us, what we feel among us.

Ciao!

"THE DESTINY OF MAN"

(Giussani's Speeches at the Spiritual Exercises of the Fraternity of Communion and Liberation, Rimini, 23–25 April 2004)

AFTER THE FIRST LESSON

This lesson by Carrón is the best thing the Lord has given me to understand in all the meetings of our Spiritual Exercises. I beg you to ask your priests, ask your leaders to give you the typescript of the tape of Fr Carrón's talk. It is the most beautiful thing I have heard in my life, the clearest, most beautiful invitation, in which the entire subject of the grace that Christ has granted us lies in the fact of that people who, in front of the things that happen in life, will make the impassioned gift of something great, great beyond compare.

I hope the Lord will give me the grace to take part in all your gatherings and to hear the meaning of things explained again as we have heard it explained today. Because, believe me – I realize I am not able to say it well, because I ought to be able to do immediately what Fr Carrón did so well just now – we want to be faithful to Christ. Faithfulness to Christ is faithfulness to the fact that the meaning of life exists, is revealed, is relevant and revealed for each one of us, in which it is impressive that the condition of life is positive, no matter what.

I am in a condition to be able to "calculate" also the contribution my experience can give to the destiny for which we were made, for which we were ordained. It is not one particular act; it is not one particular victory, but it is the true victory, which is shouting out the positivity of our life, because Christ's victory, in His death, comes from this: His reading of life as not dominated by evil, not dominated by difficult language, not described by the newness of a vocabulary, but determined in an infallible way – yes, in an infallible way – because this way is infallible, this positivity of our time, this positivity of our existence.

The fact that even a pagan is called to testify to the truth, Christ's victory in his life, is something that we shall have to remember. We must remind each other of it every day, every day we must remember the victory of wholeness, the victory of the victory, the victory of the resurrection of Christ; the victory of Christ, which will bend our hearts to being the vehicle for the knowledge that our companions in the people, our companions in the community, our companions in communion will have the right and duty to communicate to us, making of the positivity of life the salvation of what we have always wanted.

The problem is not a victory as a relief inside a death, but the meaning of death inside the fervour of a life.

I beg you to call me, to give me, as soon as you can, the opportunity to admire your faithfulness, the faithfulness of your decision, the faithfulness of your companionship, the faithfulness of our companionship, because this is the companionship that saves the world.

CLOSING WORDS
Let me greet you again. The more I reflect on it, the more I want to thank the Lord and each one of you, because the theme of this year's Exercises is the most beautiful and boundless theme imaginable. Because Christ's victory is a victory over death. And the victory over death is a victory over life. Everything has a positivity, everything is a good so intrusive that, when the Lord gives us our notice and endpoint, it will form the great suggestiveness for which this world was made.

So, there is the courage that each of us must bring for the positivity of living, so much so that any contradiction or any pain has, in the "vehicle" of this life, a positive answer.

And as a specific example, I hope we can come to a clear agreement with the Lord that He will enlighten us in everything that puts us in "new" conditions of acting, so that we may see that man's life is completely positive, profoundly positive in its final intent.

Because life is beautiful. Life is beautiful; it is a promise God made with the victory of Christ. Therefore, every day that we get out of bed – whatever our immediately perceptible, documentable situation may be, even the most painful, unimaginable – is a good that is about to be born on the edge of our horizon as men.

And we must try to translate this also into some correspondence in history. We must act so that the very history of our life is viewed as the life of all the peoples in the world, from the first all the way to the very last – as we were saying before – the very last edge of our own, of the reality which is the life of a man. Because it demands a new attention, an attention that bears within it a grand prize – the grand prize! – that bears within it already the grand prize that lies at the end of everything for every man. Where we must help each other, where we must support each other, where we must be brothers is in this ultimate positivity in the face of every pain: it is a serenity that makes our adherence serene.

And studying the history of mankind with this intent to demonstrate will be a new way to thank the ones who make us burst with joy at God's bounty, in the face of His bounty.

My best wishes to all of you, that each one of you may find on the road of your life the emergence of good which is the Risen Christ, may find the help of what awakens in man the positivity that makes it reasonable to go on living.

Praise the Lord who is victorious over death and over us! Greetings to all!

Notes

PREFACE

1 Cf. in particular L. Giussani, *L'uomo e il suo destino. In cammino [Man and His Destiny. On a Journey]* (Marietti 1820: Genoa 1999), 63–74.
2 *Ibid.*, 67.
3 Cf. Benedict XVI, Post-Synodal Apostolic Exhortation Sacramentum Caritatis, 2.
4 A. Finkielkraut, *In the Name of Humanity: Reflections on the Twentieth Century,* trans. Judith Friedlander (New York: Columbia University Press, 2000), 60.
5 C. Pavese, *This Business of Living. Diaries 1935–1950,* trans. John Taylor (Routledge, New York 2017), 33.
6 L. Giussani, *The Religious Sense* (McGill-Queen's University Press: Montreal, 1997), 108.
7 . Ratzinger, *Truth and Tolerance. Christian Belief and World Religions,* trans. Henry Taylor (Ignatius Press: San Francisco, 2004), digital edition.
8 St Augustine, *Sermo 360/B,20: Sermo sancti Augustini cum pagani ingrederentur.*

YOU OR ABOUT FRIENDSHIP

Spiritual Exercises of the Fraternity of Communion and Liberation, Rimini, 16–18 May 1997.
1 Cf. A. Savorana, *The Life of Luigi Giussani* (Montreal: McGill-Queen's University Press, 2017), 965.
2 Cf. 1 Cor 15:28 (Bible at the Vatican: www.vatican.va).

3 Cf. O.V. Milosz, *Miguel Mañara* (New York: Human Adventure Books, 2016), 89.

4 Heb 13:14 (Vatican.va).

5 Ps 8:4–5 (Vatican.va).

6 Sir 42:15.21–23; 43:28 (Vatican.va).

7 Cf. Th. Mann, *Buddenbrooks*, trans. Helen Tracy Lowe-Porter (Mineola, New York: Dover Publications Inc., 2020), Part 10, Chapter 5.

8 B. Pascal, "Thought 793," in *Thoughts Letters and Minor Works*, trans. W.F. Trotter (New York: P.F. Collier & Son Corporation, 1910), 275–276.

9 Cf. Ps 17:10–12 (Vatican.va).

10 T.S. Eliot, "Choruses from 'The Rock,'" in *Collected Poems 1909–1962*, (London: Faber and Faber, 1963), VI.

11 Cf. Ex 3:14 (Vatican.va).

12 Cf. 1 Cor 10:31; 1 Thess 5:10 (Vatican.va).

13 1 Tim 4:4 (Vatican.va).

14 Hos 10:8 (Vatican.va).

15 "*Quam multos dominos habet qui unum refugerit,*" in St Ambrose, *Epistulae extra collectionem traditae*, 14, 96.

16 Col 3:11 (Vatican.va).

17 St Maximus the Confessor, *Mystagogia*, I.

18 1 Cor 15:28 (Vatican.va).

19 Cf. Jn 17:2 (Vatican.va).

20 Cf. Jn 11:28 (Vatican.va).

21 Cf. Mt 23:8.10 (Vatican.va).

22 Cf. Lk 11:28 (Vatican.va).

23 Cf. Jn 8:44 (Vatican.va).

24 Mt 23:8 (Vatican.va).

25 Cf. Gal 6:15; 2 Cor 5:17; Ef 4:23; Col 3:9–10; Ja 1:18; 1 Pt 1:23 (Vatican.va).

26 Gal 4:4–7; cf. Rm 8:14–17.19–23; Gal 3:26 (Vatican.va).

27 Rev 21:7 (Vatican.va).

28 Cf. Ef 1:5; Eb 2:10; 12:5–8 (Vatican.va).

29 Jn 5:19–20; cf. Lk 2:49 (Vatican.va).

30 Mt 6:7–10 (Vatican.va).

31 Jn 14:6–9 (Vatican.va).

32 Cf. L. Giussani, *Alla ricerca del volto umano* (Milan: Bur, 2007), 59, 79.

33 1 Thess 5:10 (Vatican.va).

34 1 Cor 10:31 (Vatican.va).

35 Mt 5:48; cf. Lc 6:36 (Vatican.va).

36 Mt 5:18 (Vatican.va).

37 Mt 5:17 (Vatican.va).

38 1 Jn 3:3 (Vatican.va).

39 Lk 18:10–14 (Vatican.va).

40 Jn 3:16 (Vatican.va).

41 Mt 28:20 (Vatican.va).

42 Lk 23:34 (Vatican.va).

43 Jn 1:9 (Vatican.va).

44 Jn 17:6–8 (Vatican.va).

45 Rom 12:2 (Vatican.va).

46 Josef Zvěřina (1913–1990), Czech roman catholic priest, theologist, and art historian.

47 J. Zvěřina, "Letter to the Christians of the West," in L. Giussani, S. Alberto, and J. Prades, *Generating Traces in the History of the World* (Montreal: McGill-Queen's University Press, 2010), 110–112.

48 Jn 15:5 (Vatican.va).

49 L. Giussani, *Why the Church?*, trans. Viviane Hewitt (Montreal: McGill-Queen's, 2001), 189–190.

50 Lk 22:27 (Vatican.va).

51 Mt 20:28 (Vatican.va).

52 Cf. Saint Bernard, "Letter XI, To Guigues, the Prior, and to the other Monks of the Grand Chartreuse," in *Life and Works of Saint Bernard Abbot of Clairvaux*, trans. and ed. by Samuel J. Eales (London: John Hodges, 1889), 1:164–175.

53 Mt 15:24 (Vatican.va).

54 Cf. Lk 24:47 (Vatican.va).

55 Lk 13:34–35 (Vatican.va).

56 Cf. L. Giussani, "Is It Possible to Live This Way?," *Charity* (Montreal: McGill-Queen's University Press, 2009), 13.

57 Jn 18:33–37; 19:8–11 (Vatican.va).

58 Jn 11:49–52 (Vatican.va).

59 Jn 17:1–2 (Vatican.va).

60 Jn 17:3 (Vatican.va).

61 Cf. L. Giussani, *Si può (veramente?!) vivere così?* (Milan: Bur, 2020), 275 ff.

62 Cf. Heb 3,13–14 (Vatican.va).

63 Rom 13:1–3 (Vatican.va).

64 1 Pt 2:13 (Vatican.va).

65 L. Giussani, *Si può (veramente?!) vivere così?*, 420. (Our translation.)

66 Saint Catherine of Siena, *Letter to Stefano di Corrado Maconi*, n. 368.

67 Cf. Saint Catherine of Siena, *Letter to brother Bartolomeo Dominici and brother Tommaso d'Antonio*, n. 127.

68 The ancient prayer of the Angelus commemorates the Annunciation, when "the Word became flesh." (The Angel of the Lord declared unto Mary. / And she conceived of the Holy Spirit. / Behold the handmaid of the Lord. / Be it done unto me according to Thy Word. / And the Word was made flesh. / And dwells among us. / *Hail Mary …* / Pray for us, O Holy Mother of God. / That we may be made worthy of the promises of Christ // Pour forth, we beseech Thee, O Lord, Thy grace into our hearts that we to whom the incarnation of Christ Thy Son was made known by the message of an angel, may by His passion and cross be brought to the glory of His resurrection. / Through Christ our Lord. / Amen / *Glory be.*)

69 Morning prayers are the prayers (of the Liturgy of the Hours of the Catholic Church) that open the day with the psalms. These prayers characterize a communitarian personality: it is an original initiative of the individual, even in the chorus of the assembly, and it is communitarian expression, even in the solitude of one's own home. Each day of the Spiritual Exercises begins with the communal reading out of the Morning Prayers from The Book of Hours, keeping what is called the *recto tono*: it is a linear, uniform execution, in which everybody, quietly, keeps a single note.

70 Cf. Ch. Péguy, *Véronique. Dialogo della storia e dell'anima carnale* (Casale Monferrato: Piemme, 2002), 256.

71 Cf. Mt 23:8.10 (Vatican.va).

72 Cf. Lk 22:42 (Vatican.va).

73 Cf. Ef 5:2 (Vatican.va).

74 St Augustine, *Sermo 360/B,20: Sermo sancti Augustini cum pagani ingrederentur.*

75 Cf. A.J. Möhler, *Unity in the Church or the Principle of Catholicism*, trans. C. Erb (Washington, D.C: Catholic Univ. of America Press, Reprint edition, 2015), 120.

76 M. Buonarroti, *The Complete Poems of Michelangelo* (Chicago: University of Chicago Press, 2000), 150.

77 St Maximus the Confessor, *Mystagogia*, I.

THE MIRACLE OF A CHANGE

Spiritual Exercises of the Fraternity of Communion and Liberation, Rimini, 24–26 April 1998.

1 A. Savorana, *The Life of Luigi Giussani*, 999.

2 L. Giussani, *L'Uomo e il suo destino. In Cammino [Man and His Destiny: On a Journey]* (Genoa: Marietti 1820, 1999), 63.

3 J. Ratzinger cited in A. Savorana, *The Life of Luigi Giussani*, 25.

4 Cf. A. Savorana, *The Life of Luigi Giussani*, 1006.
5 L. Giussani, *In Cammino [On a Journey] (1992–1998)* (Milan: Bur, 2014), 344.
6 L. Giussani, *L'Uomo e il suo destino. In Cammino [Man and His Destiny: On a Journey]*, 63.
7 J. Ratzinger, "The Theological Locus of Ecclesial Movements," in Pontifical Council for the Laity, *Movements in the Church*. Proceedings of the World Congress of Ecclesial Movements, Rome 27 May 1998, cited in "Communio International Catholic Review," no. 3 (1998): 481.
8 L. Giussani, S. Alberto, and J. Prades, *Generating Traces in the History of the World* (Montreal: McGill-Queen's University Press, 2010), xii.
9 L. Giussani, "Milan, 3 June 1998," *The Work of the Movement. The Fraternity of Communion and Liberation* (Milan: Società Cooperativa Editoriale Nuovo Mondo, 2005), 280–281.
10 Cf. 1 Cor 15:28 (Vatican.va).
11 Cf. 1 Cor 2:12; 2 Cor 5:17; Col 1:16 (Vatican.va).
12 Cf. J. Guitton, *Arte nuova di pensare* (Cinisello Balsamo: San Paolo, 1991), 71.
13 Cf. A. Carrel, *Reflections on Life*, trans. Antonia White (London: Hamish Hamilton, 1952), 35; cf. Luigi Giussani, *The Religious Sense* (Montreal: McGill-Queen's University Press, 1997), 3.
14 Cf. L. Giussani, *The Religious Sense*, 111.
15 Quoted in A. Finkielkraut, *In the Name of Humanity: Reflections on the Twentieth Century*, trans. Judith Friedlander (New York: Columbia University Press, 2000), 60.
16 Cf. J.-P. Sartre, *Nausea*, trans. Lloyd Alexander (New York: New Directions Reprint Edition, 2013). (Our translation.)
17 Cf. Mt 5:17 (Vatican.va).
18 "Cum cognoscimus Christum, viri efficimur et iam non parvuli," cited in Victorinus Marius Africanus, *Commentarii in epistulas Pauli ad Galatas, ad Philippenses ad Ephesios*, libro II, cap. 4, v.14.
19 C. Pavese, *The Business of Living. Diaries 1935–1950*, trans. John Taylor (New York: Routledge, 2017), 33.
20 Cf. 1 Jn 5:19 (Vatican.va).
21 J. Zvěřina, "Letter to the Christians of the West," in L. Giussani, S. Alberto, and J. Prades, *Generating Traces in the History of the World*, 110–112.
22 John Paul II, message to the priests participating in a course of Spiritual Exercises promoted by Communion and Liberation, 12 September 1985, 3.

23 John Paul II, message to the Ecclesial Movements gathered on the occasion of the Second International Colloquium, 2 March 1987, 3.

24 Cf. S. Garofalo, *Il regno che non è di questo mondo* (Milan: Vita e Pensiero, 1962), 25–33.

25 Cf. Jn 14:9 (Vatican.va).

26 Cf. Jn 1:18 (Vatican.va).

27 Heb 13:8 (Vatican.va).

28 Cf. Mt 13:58 (Vatican.va).

29 J. Ratzinger, *Truth and Tolerance. Christian Belief and World Religions,* trans. Henry Taylor (San Francisco: Ignatius Press, 2004), digital edition. Part 2, chapter 1.

30 Tertullian, *De resurrectione carnis*, 8, 3: PL 2, 806.

31 J. Ratzinger, *Truth and Tolerance*. Part 2, chapter 1.

32 "*Quod natura sciebat ab aeterno, temporali didicit experimento*," cited in St Bernard, *Tractatus de gradibus humilitatis et superbiae*, cap. III, par. 6, in PL 182, col. 945.

33 Cf. Sir 39:33; 1 Tim 4:4 (Vatican.va).

34 Ch. Péguy, *Véronique*, cited in *Lui è qui* (Milan: Bur, 2009), 92. (Our translation.)

35 St Augustine, "Sermo 96,7.8," in *Sermones*, PL 38, col. 588, line 17.

36 Cf. Ch. Péguy, *Véronique. Dialogo della storia e dell'anima carnale*, 121–123. (Our translation.)

37 Cf. Ch. Péguy, *Notes on Bergson and Descartes: Philosophy, Christianity, and Modernity in Contestation*, trans. Bruce K. Ward (Eugene: Cascade Books, 2019), digital edition.

38 C. Miłosz, "Counsels," in Edward Mozejko, *Between Anxiety and Hope: The Writings and Poetry of Czeslaw Miłosz* (Edmonton: University of Alberta Press 1988), 21.

39 Cf. Jn 3:16ss (Vatican.va).

40 Cf. Jn 17:9 (Vatican.va).

41 Cf. Lk 18:8 (Vatican.va).

42 P. Claudel, *Mémoires improvisés* (Paris: Gallimard, 1954), 290. (Our translation.)

43 1 Pet 3:15 (Vatican.va).

44 Cf. Hab 2:4; Rm 1:17 (Vatican.va).

45 Cf. Mt 26:50 (Vatican.va).

46 1 Sam 16:7 (Vatican.va).

47 Lk 23:43 (Vatican.va).

48 Cf. Mt 19:29; Mk 10:30 (Vatican.va).

49 T.S. Eliot, "The Family Reunion," in *Collected Poems: 1909–1935* (New York: Harcourt, Brace and Company, 1939), http://archive.org/details/familyreunionplooelio.

50 F. Mauriac, *Saint Margaret of Cortona* (New York: Philosophical Library, 1948), 120.

51 A. Negri, *Mia giovinezza. Poesie* (Milan: Bur, 2010), 78. (Our translation.)

52 Ps 8:2–9 (Vatican.va).

53 Cf. Ps 4:9 (Vatican.va).

54 Cf. Jn 21:15–17 (Vatican.va).

55 Lk 23:34 (Vatican.va).

56 Rom 14:8 (Vatican.va).

57 Mt 18:3 (Vatican.va).

58 *"Domine Deus, in simplicitate cordis mei laetus obtuli universa. Et populum Tuum vidi, cum ingenti gaudio Tibi offerre donaria. Domine Deus, custodi hanc voluntatem cordis eorum."* Offertory prayer of the old liturgy of the feast of the Sacred Heart of Jesus, in *Messale Ambrosiano. Dalla Pasqua all'Avvento* (Milan, 1942), 225.

59 Col 1:17 (Vatican.va).

60 *"Populus Sion, ecce Dominus veniet ad salvandas gentes: et auditam faciet Dominus gloriam laudis suae in laetitia cordis vestri,"* cited in "Confractorium 4th Sunday of Advent Ambrosian Liturgy," *Messale ambrosiano. Dall'Avvento al Sabato Santo* (Milan, 1942), 78; cf. also *Vulgata,* Is 30:30.

61 Cf. Gregory of Nyssa, *The Life of Moses,* in PG 44: 377B; Id.; *"Homily XII"* on the *Song of Songs,* in PG 44: 10280.

62 Cf. Mt 18:3 (Vatican.va).

CHRIST IS ALL AND IN ALL

Spiritual Exercises of the Fraternity of Communion and Liberation, Rimini, 23–25 April 1999.

1 L. Giussani, "Reason Versus Power," from *la Repubblica,* 24 October 1998, translated in *30Days,* no. 10 (1998): 60.

2 L. Giussani, "Letter Sent to John Paul II on the 50th Anniversary of CL's Beginning," in A. Savorana, *The Life of Luigi Giussani,* 1119.

3 Opening prayer of the Mass of Monday in Holy Week, *Roman Missal.*

4 Ps 32 (31):9 (Vatican.va).

5 A. Carrel, *Reflections on Life,* trans. Antonia White (London: Hamish

Hamilton, 1952), 35; cf. L. Giussani, *The Religious Sense* (Montreal: McGill-Queen's University Press, 1997), 3.

6   L. Giussani, *The Religious Sense*, 10.

7   Ps 139:13–16 (Vatican.va).

8   Ps 8:5–6 (Vatican.va).

9   Cf. St Augustine, *De Genesi ad litteram libri duodecim*, IV, 33; IX, 17, 20; cf. also St Augustine *Confessions*, XIII, 4; *De Trinitate Dei*, III, 8,13; 9,16; VI 7,8; *De Civitate Dei contra Paganos*, XI, 21; XII, 2.

10   Ps 8:7–9 (Vatican.va).

11   N.A. Berdyaev, *The Realm of Spirit and the Realm of Caesar*, trans. Donald A. Lowrie (New York: Harper, 1953), 40.

12   H. Arendt, *Lavoro, opera, azione. Le forme della vita attiva* (Verona: Ombre corte, 1997), 70. (Our translation.)

13   Jn 8:43–44 (Vatican.va).

14   Ez 20:24–25 (Vatican.va).

15   F.W. Nietzsche, "Thus Spoke Zarathustra," in *Cambridge Texts in the History of Philosophy*, trans. Adrian Del Caro (Cambridge, Mass.: Cambridge University Press, 2011), 51.

16   H. Arendt, *La lingua materna* (Milan: Mimesis, 2005), 77. (Our translation.)

17   Cf Ps 14:1, Ps 53:2 (Vatican.va).

18   A. Camus, *Notebooks 1942–1951*, trans. Justin O'Brien (Open Library, Ivan R. Dee, 2010), 199.

19   *Ibid.*

20   Jn 17:9 (Vatican.va).

21   H. Arendt, *The Life of the Mind*, (New York: Harcourt Brace Jovanovich, 1978), 157.

22   H. Arendt, *The Jewish Writings* (New York: Schocken Books, 2007), 378.

23   M. Luzi, *L'inferno e il limbo*, ilSaggiatore, Milano 1964, 17. (Our translation.)

24   Cf. Ex 34:5–6 (Vatican.va).

25   M. Buber, *The Way of Man: According to Hasidic Teaching* (Wallingford: Pendle Hill Publications, 2002), 30.

26   Is 55:8 (Vatican.va).

27   Jer 6:16 (Vatican.va).

28   Dt 32:7 (Vatican.va).

29   Wis 9:15 (Vatican.va).

30   Dt 6:4–9 (Vatican.va).

31   Cf. L. Giussani, *At the Origin of the Christian Claim* (Montreal: McGill-Queen's Univeristy Press, 1998).

32 Gen 17:1–3 (Vatican.va).

33 J. Roth, *The Wandering Jews* (New York: W.W. Norton, 2001), 27–28.

34 Gen 17:4.6–7 (Vatican.va).

35 Dt 7:7–8 (Vatican.va).

36 Dt 30:11–14 (Vatican.va).

37 Jn 10:30 (Vatican.va).

38 A. Camus, *Notebooks 1935–1942*, trans. Philip Thody (New York: Knopf, 1963), 174.

39 Ch. Péguy, "Un nouveau théologien, M. Fernand Laudet," *Cahiers de la Quinzaine*, no. 2, vol. XIII, 25 September 1911, also cited in *Charles Péguy, Oeuvres en prose complètes*, vol. III (Paris: Gallimard, 1992), 573–574. (Our translation.)

40 G. Gaber, "*Canzone dell'appartenenza*," from the record *Un'idiozia conquistata a fatica 98–99*, © GIOM, 1999. (Our translation.)

41 P.A. Florensky, *The Pillar and Ground of the Truth*, trans. Boris Jakim (Princeton: Princeton University Press, 2004), 54, 55.

42 Eph 1:4–5 (Vatican.va).

43 Rom 8:9 (Vatican.va).

44 Cf. Dionisius the Areopagite, *De Divinis Nominibus*, XI, 5, 953 A.

45 St Augustine, *Tractatus in Iohannis evangelium*, II, 4, 40.

46 St Irenaeus of Lyons, *Adversus Haereses*, III, 20, 2.

47 St Bernard, *Sermo primus in Epiphania Domini*, 1–2.

48 2 Cor 5:14–15 (Vatican.va).

49 Rom 14:7–8 (Vatican.va).

50 Gal 2:20 (Vatican.va).

51 Eph 2:10 (Vatican.va).

52 This refers to the meeting of the Holy Father John Paul II with the ecclesial movements and new communities, St Peter's Square, Rome, 30 May 1998. Cf. L. Giussani, S. Alberto, and J. Prades, *Generating Traces in the History of the World*, IX–XII.

53 Cf. H. Ibsen, *Brand*, trans. F.E. Garret (New York: E.P. Dutton and Co., n.d.), 223.

54 Saint Therese of Lisieux, *The Story of a Soul. The Autobiography of The Little Flower*, trans. Michael Day (Charlotte: TAN Books, 2010), digital edition.

55 Gen 22:17 (Vatican.va).

56 Paul VI, "The Projection of the Holy Year in the Future of the Church," 23 July 1975, in *L'Osservatore Romano*, 25 July 1975, 1.

57 St Fulgentius of Ruspe, *Ad Monimum libri III*, II, 11–12.

58 T.S. Eliot, "Choruses from 'The Rock,'" in *Collected Poems 1909–1962*, (London: Faber and Faber, 1963), 175.

59 Cf. Jn 17:1–10; Mt 11:27; Lk 10:22; Jn 16:15 (Vatican.va).
60 Rev 3:15–17 (Vatican.va).
61 Lk 18:8 (Vatican.va).
62 1 Thess 5:9–11;16–21 (Vatican.va).
63 Opening prayer Saturday, fifth week of Lent "In traditione symboli" (Ambrosian Rite), in *Messale ambrosiano quotidiano. Tempo di Avvento, Natale, Quaresima, Pasqua*, I.
64 Cf. F.W. Nietzsche, "Thus Spoke Zarathustra," 51.
65 Rm 14:7–8 (Vatican.va).
66 St Gregory Nazianzen, *Carmina*, II/I, carme LXXIV, 4–12, in PG 38: 1421–1422.
67 Cf. Lk 7:11–17 (Vatican.va).

SPEECHES AND GREETINGS

1   L. Giussani, "The Blow to the Heart," *Traces: Litterae communionis*, no. 11 (2003).
2   L. Giussani, "The Gamble of God's Power in Time," *Traces: Litterae communionis*, no. 1 (2005).
3   C. Pavese, *This Business of Living. Diaries, 1935–1950* (New York: Routledge, 2017), 55.
4   L. Giussani cited in A. Savorana, *The Life of Luigi Giussani*, 1146.
5   C. Chieffo, "Io non sono degno," in *Canti*, (Milan: Società Cooperativa Editoriale Nuovo Mondo, 2014), 201–2.
6   M. Campi and A. Mascagni, "Povera voce," in *Canti*, 208.
7   Jn 13:30 (Vatican.va).
8   C. Chieffo, "Ballata del potere," in *Canti*, 219–20.
9   *Ibid.*
10 Cf. Lk 7:11–16 (Vatican.va).
11 Lk 7:13 (Vatican.va).
12 Irenaeus of Lyons, *Adversus haereses*, IV, 20,7.